Sweet
Nothings

Also by Sarah Perry

After the Eclipse

Sweet Nothings

Confessions of a Candy Lover

Sarah Perry

With illustrations by Forsyth Harmon

MARINER BOOKS

New York   Boston

SWEET NOTHINGS. Copyright © 2025 by Sarah Perry. Illustrations copyright © Forsyth Harmon. All rights reserved. Printed in the United States of America. No part of this book may be used or reproduced in any manner whatsoever without written permission except in the case of brief quotations embodied in critical articles and reviews. For information, address HarperCollins Publishers, 195 Broadway, New York, NY 10007.

HarperCollins books may be purchased for educational, business, or sales promotional use. For information, please email the Special Markets Department at SPsales@harpercollins.com.

The Mariner flag design is a registered trademark of HarperCollins Publishers LLC.

FIRST EDITION

Designed by Chloe Foster

Library of Congress Cataloging-in-Publication Data has been applied for.

ISBN 978-0-06-331992-9

24 25 26 27 28 LBC 5 4 3 2 1

To Preston—the sweetest one.

"A multitude of small delights constitute happiness."
—CHARLES BAUDELAIRE

"Happiness . . . not in another place but this place, not for another hour but this hour."
—WALT WHITMAN, *Leaves of Grass*

"Sometimes I think that the thing I love most about being an adult is the right to buy candy whenever and wherever I want."
—RYAN GOSLING

Contents

Sweet
Nothings

Introduction

On Root Beer Barrels

J ust an elegant idea, these—an intensely sugary soda in nugget form. The shape of this ancient penny candy is so old-fashioned I wonder if it makes any sense to kids these days, when and if they encounter it. Even in the 1980s, barrels abounded in my childhood, on-screen and in person: they carried cartoon characters over waterfalls, and they stood in the rock shop near my home in Maine, filled with tiny polished stones that my mother and I dipped our arms into, the cool, smooth surfaces flowing over our skin. Barrels decorated restaurants in the mountains of New Hampshire, where my aunt Gwen lived, where everything rustic had a clean, burnished charm. Barrel planters bordered yards, standing vertical or artfully tipped over, spilling pansies and marigolds onto bright lawns surrounded by tall pines.

I would get my root beer barrels from the penny candy counter at our tiny Main Street pharmacy, which tells you what a time capsule Maine is, its people forever looking backward, visiting drive-ins and roadside ice cream stands, using all manner of old language to help and confuse those "from away." (Ask directions of a Mainer—and you will have to, because cell reception is abysmal up there—and those directions will include at least one landmark that hasn't stood there for a decade, or the name of a family farm now paved over with a Dollar General.) Those sugar barrels were admirably detailed: little incised lines for the planks, two raised rings for the stays. Wait, that's not right: the wooden boards are called staves, the metal rings that hold them together are hoops. I used to have this knowledge: *staves, hoops, bilge*— it comes back to me, and I wonder how much other forgotten knowledge I contain. As kids we'd giggle at "bunghole," even before *Beavis and Butt-Head*. Those were days of analog knowledge, when the thought of wood entered the daily conversation, when at least some of the materials of your life would be recognizable to your ancestors. Before everything became plastic, acrylic, ahistorical.

So this candy was an ancient shape, echoing an object that stood in distilleries and barns and in the holds of ships made from the same wood and iron, and the flavor, too, was old, a treat crafted for your great-grandparents. The base for root beer is sarsaparilla or sassafras, long known to the region's Native American peoples as medicine, commodified by white pharmacists in the mid-nineteenth century, enhanced with various herbs and spices. Birch, spruce, wintergreen: a forest on the tongue, the depth of old-growth trees entering your body, ushered in by sugar. Star anise, nutmeg, clove, ginger: spices that had once been precious, once meant wealth. Molasses: currency and history, the South and its violence, the North and its violence.

Maine takes its soda several steps further in its preference for Moxie, a darker brown sweet beverage with a flavor usually

described, inadequately, as "root beer plus cough medicine." Moxie dates to 1876—the same year Charles Elmer Hires created the first commercial root beer. It was first marketed as a medicine called Moxie Nerve Food—meant to cure anything from "softening of the brain" to "nervousness"—before the company added carbonation, making it one of the most popular soft drinks in America. It has a bitter aftertaste, a long kick that attacks as soon as the liquid vacates your mouth, fuming out your nostrils. Many Mainers love this sensation, and still others, like me, will themselves to love it out of some desire to belong. Or perhaps we go back for another sip simply because the first hit of sweetness is the only way to dispel the aftertaste. Sweetness and bubbles, bitter fumes, sweetness, repeat until gone, like living through one hellish icy winter after another, the few crisp, bright days of summer a reprieve just long enough to let amnesia settle in, to keep you from moving away. To drink Moxie you need moxie, the synonym for chutzpah named after the drink America forgot.

This bittersweet liquid is locked into the state identity and given its own festival each summer, one I'm glad David Foster Wallace didn't cast his shadow upon. Unlike lobsters and pine trees and Stephen King, Moxie is something that constitutes them—us—that the flatlanders don't know much about. It lives in the state psyche alongside the potato fields in the counties up north, where kids still, two decades into the twenty-first century, get weeks off school for the harvest. We dig in the dirt for the food that went wrong back in Ireland (even though the starvation really came courtesy of English rule), the old country many of us left to wedge ourselves between rocks on land that rightfully should still belong to the Wabanaki and Abenaki among us, and we sip a drink that provides a flash second of enjoyment followed by bitterness, and we are proud. We buy Moxie whenever we see it at the gas station, driving the narrow roads split apart and buckled by frost heaves, winter perpetually with us even in summer, sipping it as we wind around mountains and along the shores of lakes, no logical, direct path from one place to another, because, as we say, *you can't get there from here.* You can, but it takes some doing. Here's a bitter drink for your journey, one meant to cure whatever ails you.

I just discovered that the thing that gives Moxie its bitter flavor—and I hadn't expected it to be a single ingredient, thought it would be a complex, varying blend, like root beer or Chartreuse—is gentian root. Aperol—so trendy in cocktails these past few years—also contains gentian. But gentian, for me, is gentian violet, a blazingly bright purple liquid that carried me through some of my most difficult recent years.

At perhaps the high point of my life, the release of my first book, a memoir titled *After the Eclipse,* my body broke down, stress and huge emotions finally taking their toll after six years of writing. The book is about my mother's life and her sudden, violent death. She worked hard as a single mother, devoting herself to me and to a search for true love, until she was murdered in our home by a stranger when she was thirty and I was twelve. The task of transforming all that darkness into something meaningful and life-affirming had been monumental, and I could not, at first, imagine what could come next. After years of trying to make my life about more than just my most painful loss, I had moved back into that story, become publicly defined by it. I found myself wondering what happens once we've survived, how we make meaning of all the days that come after the end of the dramatic story. I was so tired of darkness. Maybe my next book, I told my friends, should be about kittens and rainbows. I didn't know how accurate that joke would prove to be.

Back then, I was honored to have written that book, to have been able to, and honored that hundreds of people were coming out to events in six states to hear me read from it, but I was also overwhelmed. Most overwhelmed was my pussy, which caught perhaps only my second yeast infection ever, one that started so suddenly and got such a strong hold on me that at first I didn't even recognize it for what it was. When the first doctor assured me that I was not, in fact, dying of some rare disease, I was relieved, having no idea how long I would suffer. I'll spare further details, but trust me, you never want to be medically interesting.

Back in the early days of my memoir's publication, I suffered, too full of vicious microbes for the usual magic-bullet pill to even work. I was told the condition was localized, but I could feel it was systemic. No pills, no creams, no suppositories (terrible word)—nothing—worked. The pills had no effect whatsoever, powerless pink pellets thrown into a volcano. The creams burned me, something I was told wasn't possible, even as I experienced it, trying to sleep while blowtorches tore my insides on the nights when I tried them once again, desperate and foolishly hopeful.

My life at that time was supposedly about witness, about testimony, and this should have been when my word meant the most—my word, after all, was what engendered all those bookstore gatherings—and yet in the privacy of the exam room I was disregarded. I was continually told that I was somehow causing my own pain. Doctor after doctor told me to do things I was already doing to soothe symptoms they insisted I wasn't having. One told me to eat more salad, at a time when I had in fact been eating an unusual amount of salad, so concerned was I with my image, so driven was I to be a perfect, pleasing vessel for story, thin and beautiful like my mother had been. "It's immunological," said another doctor, offering an encouragingly serious word, but when I asked further questions—about what she meant exactly, or what the word meant for my treatment—I could ascertain nothing further. Should I go to an immunologist, then? I asked. Or an endocrinologist? Or . . . some other -ologist? She shrugged, flapped a hand at me in an *I wouldn't bother* gesture, and sent me on my way with the same useless little pill that had failed me before. Each doctor seemed to think their prescription pad contained some magic fairy dust that would make the pill work this time.

I traveled from state to state, visiting every place I had lived over the years. My whole body constantly burned with a slight fever, and I was weak, and I lost more weight, and I smiled and hugged and kissed cheeks and focused hard on all that love to ignore the terrible discomfort below. My face was constantly red, and in photos I can see I overdid it with the green color-correcting concealer, giving myself a zombielike pallor. I could not wear my uniform of black jeans, I could not drink, I could not have sex, I could not have dairy, I could not have carbs, I could not eat sugar. No sugar, none: I felt the effects instantly, although every doctor told me, of course, that this was impossible. A treat as tiny as a single root beer barrel was unthinkable, a reckless indulgence not worth the punishment. I was entirely stripped of all my pleasurable coping mechanisms. Even worse, in the absence of authoritative evidence, I'd had to impose these restrictions on myself, so what should have been a victory lap felt more like a parade of self-abnegation. My friends offered me champagne and cakes, knowing my passion for both, and old lovers came out and leaned in close and asked me to come home with them after my events, and I had to turn it all down. I found myself alone and burning in hotel rooms, in silence, with salad.

In each city I got worse, cramped airplanes and humid car rides turning out to be where candida most loves to party, and in each city I visited a doctor, delicately negotiating the logistics with hosts and friends of varying levels of intimacy, tiptoeing awkwardly around the need for a ride or tearfully revealing to them my condition in the hope that they would make calls to their own gynecologists. Finally, at home in Maine, a beautiful, generous young doctor who'd slipped me in between appointments (a friend of my kind host, Joan) recommended gentian violet. "It's a liquid you apply," she said, "but the thing is, it'll turn you all purple." The purple lasts a week or so after every application. By then it had been weeks since I'd heard any new ideas. A new idea meant hope. "Yes, please, give it to me," I said. "I don't care about being purple." Who could care about that? I was aghast at the provincial vanity of anyone who would refuse relief because it would tint them with color. I was fully ready to become an O'Keeffe petunia. Maybe now I could finally stop googling, get off WebMD, get things under control enough so the fucking arugula could work its magic.

The young doctor left the exam room for a while and my heart calmed. Relief would come soon. My love for her radiated out to the entire building, the town, the world. I even sent forgiveness to the Salad Doctor; doctoring was a hard job, after all, and now I would be well, no harm done. The young doctor returned in ten or so minutes, said the office had discarded its last dose of gentian violet when it expired— it'd been so long since anyone had used this treatment. It was super old-fashioned, what Russian grandmothers used, I would later learn. That I was hearing about it at all was a testament to Maine's anachronism. I burst into tears as suddenly as a child fallen on a sidewalk. I was as heartbroken as if she'd told me they'd thrown out the last bottle on the planet. The medicine was never coming, and I would keep burning and suffering and starving, sitting alone and half-naked on scratchy paper on vinyl tables up and down the Eastern Seaboard, telling story after story about a mom who was never coming back.

I apologized through my tears as the doctor told me about a natural foods store that was likely to have the royal liquid in stock. She was incredibly kind; when I couldn't stop weeping, she called them for me to check. "They'll have a bottle set aside for you," she finally said. "They're on Forest Avenue." She gave me a bouquet of six-inch cotton swabs. "Put this in the liquid and then swirl it around inside you," she said. "Be careful: it is very purple and will stain everything it touches." She wasn't kidding: one tiny speck easily turns into a banner of color, radiant like a springtime bloom. I would spend the next couple of months secretly bleach-cleaning the bathrooms of each friend and family member who took me in on my travels.

At the natural foods store, I found a man standing at a long, carved-wood counter, with various teas and tinctures in glass jars gleaming on long shelves behind him, each a promise of health, the whole picture recalling that old penny candy counter at my hometown pharmacy. As he handed me the little bottle of purple, I wanted to express my gratitude, but I didn't want to refer to my condition, embarrassing as it was. I was finding that my usual body and sex positivity evaporated when the body in question was mine and it was vulnerable. To write a memoir is to decide to reveal secrets and intimacies, but the forced disclosures of sickness are something else entirely.

Sweating with newfound hope, I swirled as the doctor had instructed in a coffee shop bathroom on my way to a newspaper interview on my way to a reading where I met the extremely famous writer Richard Russo, who had read my book and complimented its structure, which had been the book's biggest challenge. I have a picture of us together that Joan took sneakily and sent to me in a frame that now hangs in my office. He's wearing a corduroy jacket with elbow patches, and I look infinitely less terrible than I felt, standing there in my favorite polka-dotted shirt and a can't-believe-my-luck smile. I also had a cold that day, and my voice was ragged and quiet, but the bookstore was incredibly cozy, and the owner gave me one of the best, most thoughtful introductions I received on the whole tour. The gentian violet cooled me, and I applied more when I got home to Joan's, more every chance I got, and my royal-purple pussy soon healed enough that the pills finally worked. There was an astounding rightness to this: the bitter root that gives my hometown drink its bite had healed me via a strangely beautiful transformation. The flora of Maine had given me what I needed when I most needed it; the land where I'd experienced my greatest loss had finally made some grand gesture of penance.

But the thing about examining both our joys and our struggles is that we so often find that ideas we'd held sacred turn out to be false. I recently learned that my magical purple potion is named for the vivid color of *Gentiana verna*—which is used to flavor Moxie—but that it doesn't contain anything of the plant itself. It's made in a lab, a chemical by-product of coal tar, its safety questionable enough to get it banned in Canada and Australia.

But I can't help it: the otherworldly, candy-colored vial underneath my bathroom sink still feels miraculous to me, fated. The other name for gentian violet is crystal violet—my mother's name, paired with the flower she scattered around our house in little pots, scrappy plants with velvet leaves and furled petals, smelling of tangy, bitter earth. And it's still true that I was saved by this old medicine from my home state, by my people's willingness to hold on to the past. I had wanted a pure connection, but what I had instead was a story—a little sweet, a little bitter.

Chewy Reds

On Strawberry Rip Rolls

I received this as a gift from my dear friends Alan Michael and Daniel, who purchased it from a dollar store near Holden Beach, North Carolina, a small, undeveloped town hugging the curve at the bottom of the state. This neat roll of tape calls to mind both Fruit Roll-Ups and Bubble Tape gum, and it is thus a guaranteed nostalgia generator for a nineties kid. I ate this on a beach and welcomed the tactile experience, the messy fun of pulling and stretching and breaking it. The roll is nestled in a crimped plastic package—nothing special, nothing like the cool measuring-tape dispenser of Bubble Tape, but at least it opens easily, the plastic quickly yielding, breaking as though brittle. The candy tape is bright red, almost hot pink, and covered in futuristic sugar crystals. The tape's surface is intricately ribbed, calling to mind another object that, days later, I still can't place. At first I thought of correction tape, the old-fashioned kind for typewriters, but that's not right—that didn't have texture. I keep picturing a grooved beige strip. I might be thinking of a belt deep inside a printer that I tangled with at my first desk job. This physical

rhyme will trouble me until the memory, like memories will, suddenly clicks into place. I can wait.

The tape breaks easily, which is a plus, coming apart with a slight stretch followed by a satisfying snap. The sugar is grainy on the tongue, which is interesting but off-putting in this particular venue. On a beach, it's too much like sand. Smaller grains would give this the sparkle-melt feeling they were likely going for without grinding between the teeth.

The flavor itself is a disappointment. Red is usually the clear winner in a colorful candy, even if it doesn't taste like the strawberry or raspberry or cherry it aspires to be. Red is excitement and brightness and I'm here for it. This red exactly matches the aroma of children's strawberry shampoo, which as a kid you end up tasting a little bit as the overexcited foam gets washed into the corners of your mouth, before you've perfected your signature of nuanced head tilts and hair flicks that will prevent you from eating it, the pattern of personal grooming that, when you finally stand in a shower with a lover, will look like the mating dance of an exotic bird.

Tasting this, I'm five again, using that shampoo and standing below my mother, who must have started me on showers with supervision. I'm asking if I can stay a few minutes longer, "to relax," as she guides the suds that I missed out of my hair. She grants me these few minutes, stepping out so I can stand under the water alone, tipping back my head and shutting my eyes, the warmth deep in my body. I might have gotten the idea of needing to relax from ambient exposure to her stress, but the important thing is that she allows me these moments, even if the strain on the water heater will drive up the electricity bill, because relaxing and pleasure are valued in this house. It will take me a long time to understand that not everyone was raised like this. This ethos will bring me to this beach, with these kind friends, will lead me to prioritize a whole week of sunshine, year after year. Other friends will say, every year, "Wow, a whole week?" Yes, a whole week. Of course, it's a huge privilege to be able to do this. My mother herself could not have pulled it off—not a whole week, not right on the dunes.

What confounds me is that people question why one would want to take a week and lie on a towel, idle except for the occasional lazy turn of a paperback page. It's as though they can't imagine allowing themselves. Sustaining pleasure is, after all, a skill—maybe even a responsibility, if we are to remain joyous enough to be good to one another.

Under that radiant beach sunshine, I take another bite of the tape candy, considering this flavor-aroma echo. Could they use the same chemical additive for shampoo and for candy—would that be legal? Is that why this ended up at a dollar store in rural North Carolina? It's not a good candy, but it's candy, and the sugar grains propel me to another few bites. Also, it's a gift, so I feel I should give it my best shot.

Alan Michael informs me that I don't have to finish it, and because everyone's watching me, I do the sensible thing and put the rest back in the package, to be thrown away up at the house. Later, since I would be embarrassed to be seen eating something I've declared to be garbage, I write about this candy as a way of prolonging the experience. The next day, I write about another. And another.

On Twizzlers

I have pure love for Twizzlers, and I also love how much other people love them. When I'm driving, I always prefer the radio to hooking up my own music: knowing that thousands of other people are out there, hearing the same songs and singing along, all of us strangers breathing in time, our bodies infused with the same drumbeat, makes everything sound better. And so with Twizzlers, a candy that inspires devotion.

This may leave you wondering if Twizzlers are my favorite candy. Sugar is a pleasure that I take seriously. I have rhapsodized about the perfection of a fresh Twix and tipsily ranted about how overrated Trader Joe's Peanut Butter Cups are. But I can't answer this "favorite" question, not yet. The underlying

premise—that our strongest desires are stable, unchangeable, that we crown a best love and leave it at that—depresses me. Pleasure is wonderfully circumstantial, varied. Favorite under what circumstances? In what weather? On the road or at home? In what mood? Can I get my hands dirty? My fellow candy people understand, but hopefully we all have something that lights us up, gives us a reprieve, some kind of tactile, visceral experience that keeps us connected to the world and about which we're a little obsessive. For some it's sports, yoga, gardening, or sex; for me it's candy—and sex, though not at the same time. More on that later.

Twizzlers are for sitting on picnic tables on green lawns with sprinklers running, the tiny, suspended globes of water disappearing in the summer heat before they hit the ground. Twizzlers are for cool, dark movie theaters, barely visible in the light reaching you and your boyfriend, sitting way at the back, where you alternate the pleasures of kissing and chewing. Twizzlers aren't a gas station candy, but they're a road trip candy: pair with a cooler of sodas and plastic-wrapped sandwiches, and ration each piece—each stick? each twizz?—to make the package last the two-day drive.

I can't continue without addressing the obnoxious chorus I can already hear, the "But have you had Red Vines?" people. Are they Canadian, these people? Is the candy? Or is it American regional? I don't know. The point is they miss the point. Red Vines are nice, sure. They are softer and they have a brighter flavor. But Twizzlers are iconic. *Parks and Recreation*'s Leslie Knope was right to wonder if Twizzlers people and Red Vines people can marry—even the Red Vines brand manager cites the Montagues and Capulets in speaking of the rivalry.

I'm tired of this foodie business where we compare classic

snacks with lesser-known or bespoke versions of same. Yes, the homemade pop tarts at Little Zelda coffee shop on Franklin Avenue are mind-bogglingly good. I first had one when I wandered in there, my first week in Brooklyn, more than a decade ago. How could a coffee shop be so small, such a perfect little jewel, dominated by its gigantic Italian espresso maker, floor in half-inch tiles, walls covered with printed flyers and notices and notes from customers, like it was the 1990s? How could a barista be so kind while trapped in that tiny box? How the fuck did someone make a pop tart so delicious? The crust was flaky, the strawberry filling tasted like a meadow, the frosting melted onto your tongue and off the pastry instead of snapping like a crust or falling to crumbles. It was a food moment I'll remember all my life, one I repeated semiweekly for the next few weeks. But were these homemade pastries better than actual Pop-Tarts? No. And can you get a perfect coffee shop pastry on your way home at 3 a.m. after leaving a dear friend's birthday party, blanketed in a weed high sparkled with remnants of champagne? No. Not even in Brooklyn, and so, not anywhere. A block or so from your apartment, you'll steer yourself into the bigger bodega, the one that's open all night, the one with grocery store aspirations. You'll trawl the tiny aisles, a leaning ship of want, and when you see that familiar box, the name leaping out in one of the world's more enthusiastic fonts, the little kid in you, the kindergartner, has just opened her lunch box and discovered all over again how much her mother loves her. Here is the unadorned silver packet. Two just for you. Chewy and satisfying even when you can't toast them.

So, Red Vines. Cute, okay. Enjoy them in earnest Canada

or the Upper Peninsula of Michigan or Big Sur or wherever. That's not what we're talking about here.

Twizzlers have that phase-change advantage of all candies that alter in the heat or cold without getting ruined. On hot days they are gummier, just this side of sticky, extra luxurious. As you hand one to your friend, it bends in a limp arc, offering a silly dick joke. You can giggle a little even if neither of you says anything. A limp Twizzler stretching from hand to hand is a reminder that the appendage is ridiculous, that humans are ridiculous. We're eating refined corn syrup and synthetic coloring here, but look at how joyous, look at this miracle, think of the very name of this thing—what Mad Men genius dreamed that up? The bubbling joy of a swizzle stick in a cocktail, the pure uselessness of spinning around until you're dizzy, the preadolescent magnetic storm of subliminal sexual tension in a game of Twister. Twizzlers. Brilliant.

It's an abundant candy. Even for a candy devotee like me, there isn't that feeling of scarcity that usually accompanies sugar. It's okay and common to buy them in big bags. The size of the stick is just right for nibbling, so it takes a minute to take one down. Then you reach in and peel the next from where it spoons with its neighbors, disconnecting it as if opening a zipper, expanding the moment between want and satisfaction. You nibble again. Go back in there, pull another. You still haven't had a lot of candy, volume-wise. Twizzlers helped me transition from a miserable fifth grader whose nickname was "Heifer" to the seventh grader I see now in pictures: lovely defined collarbones; long, straight, perfectly nineties middle-parted hair; skin clear as a child's but glowing with first hormones.

In colder weather, Twizzlers firm up, get chewier, more like the black licorice they're modeled on. (I wonder if these first strawberry licorices struck consumers as bizarro abominations, similar to how I regard Key Lime Pie Kit Kat today.) They get harder to pull from one another, and there's a tiny pleasure in the violence of separating each one from its peers, in peeling it cleanly off without breaking it. The twisted ridges press into the soft organ of your tongue, surrounded by cloudy exhalations. It's good to have to work infinitesimally harder for the satisfaction, especially if you're a person whose sense of pleasure is sharpened by effort and waiting, as I am, as many are, as most are if they're honest, if they pay attention.

How do they taste? Does it really matter?

On Pop Rocks

What ever possessed the candymakers of the late twentieth century? It was an era when strange textures and intense physical sensations predominated, a sort of arms race to see who could devise the weirdest way to mainline sugar. By the 1990s we had Pixy Stix and Ring Pops and Nerds and Fun Dip. Fun Dip! Just a bag of finely ground sugar, really, pastel cocaine. I once read a charmingly shocked account of a child rubbing the last grains of Fun Dip onto her gums, and I believe it. The nineties provided more textures than you could dream of, more ways to consume sugar than seemed possible, and kids were ready to make new rituals. A lot of the candies of the era prioritized immediacy, and we loved getting the sugar direct—a straight shot to the bloodstream—riding that swift boost recognized by dance and pageant moms today,

who readily admit on online message boards to pouring Pixys into their little competitors before showtime.

The most lauded of these structurally weird candies is, of course, Pop Rocks. They come in a little black packet and the first step is to take the top edge firmly between thumb and forefinger (nondominant hand) and wave it while flicking at the bottom with a middle finger violently unfurled from your thumb. You've seen your mother do this to sugar packets when she gets coffee at McDonald's. The idea is to get all of the candy grains into the bottom half so that when you rip off the top you lose as little as possible to spillage. It also looks cool and adult and like a drug ritual, which it is.

Flicking done—don't overdo it or you won't look cool anymore—tear as directed. Inside is a sparkling, jewel-toned heap of crystals, irregular, translucent rocks that resemble crystal meth. The idea is to pour the stuff directly into your maw, where the jagged chunks will pop on contact with your saliva, flying sharply around inside your soft little face.

Mom gave me my first packet when I was seven, and I remember, as I tried it out, watching her face while she watched mine. She was delighted to share an experience from her childhood, and I knew her happiness would come in direct proportion to how much I liked it. I often had this sensation as a child, particularly when I was engaging in some public ritual designed to be fun. Theme parks made me nervous, because I had trouble losing myself, could always feel the gap between the expected glee and my performance of it. The McDonald's ball pit was the worst, a thunderdome of parental expectation, bumping into sticky strangers in the plastic surf while trying to ignore the ring of adults around us, their faces twisted into overlarge smiles, their fingers grasping the netted boundary like claws, willing us to feel happy. But enjoying candy was easy, interior, uncomplicated. Standing there before my mother, I held the rocks on my tongue and waited, and soon—ping! A tiny explosion against the back of my right front tooth. My eyebrows shot up, my eyes went wide. "Oh!" I said as more little bursts released on my tongue, on my palate, accented by smaller sparkles like needling rain. Mom giggled, clapped her hands together. "So cool!" I finally said, before eagerly pouring more into the cave of my mouth.

Later I would hear the rumors: Mikey, the Life cereal kid, had died when he combined Coke with Pop Rocks. The carbonations had multiplied, exploding his stomach. We kids all imagined the worst tummy ache we'd ever had, times a zillion. The Mikey story would cling, predisposing me to a fear of appendicitis, which in my no-insurance twenties hovered like a threat: a terrible way to die, go bankrupt, or both. I didn't trust myself to decide my pain was bad enough in time to go to the hospital before the organ burst. We want to believe that we can worry our way to safety, that surely we'll see major diseases like cancer coming, that we can just avoid risky activities like, say, waterskiing and we'll be just fine. Appendicitis, though. What even is it?

Anyway, the Mikey story implied that he should've known better. He was a reckless hedonist—a TV star, after all—and so Pop Rocks and Coke became a morality tale about greed. But even if you weren't planning on ingesting that particular eight ball, death by candy had now joined the pantheon of childhood worries, along with quicksand and getting your tongue stuck on an icy pole and disappointing your mother. What if you were watching a movie, distracted, and still had some of those tiny candy jewels in your mouth, and then took a big swig of your friend's Coke, which had been sitting there next to you, sweating lusciously onto your elbow? What then? Would you die from such a simple mistake? Was it really that easy to be taken down, was the world so full of dangers, even from the things that should have given us happiness?

I remember sitting on the swings when I was eight or nine, thinking back to my mother giving me my first Pop Rocks, but now I felt betrayed. Why hadn't she warned me? How had she just stood there, smiling, giving me a taste for something that could kill me?

Years later, I would feel guilty for believing the world over her. Of course, the rumors were untrue. Mikey was alive and well and, according to his mom, "the only one truly enjoying Pop Rocks, knowing that he wasn't dead." But on my playground, kids were still trading packets of the stuff, which had picked up an illicit allure.

General Foods, the makers of Pop Rocks, had tried to get Mikey to appear in commercials for them, but he was locked into an exclusive contract with Life, a pretty elegant state of affairs for a kid presumed dead. Although the candy would be resurrected by another company three years later, General Foods eventually gave up on debunking the rumors, crushing their remaining stock of Pop Rocks—300 million packets' worth—with a steamroller and burying it underground, proving that even unfounded fears can be terribly destructive.

On Swedish Fish

No one's discerning enough about Swedish Fish. Listen, there are two kinds, or two kinds of red ones. Yes, there are multicolor packs, with orange and green and yellow fish, but those aren't nearly as good. We won't bother with them here.

The more common, larger Swedish Fish are about the length of a thumb, semitransparent, with a soft bite like any other molded chewy candy: dinosaurs, worms, sub-Haribo-quality bears. They're fine. They're red but not deep red, cute-ish but not adorable; the chew is okay but not distinctive. Eating these, I remove the tails first, neatly nipping off the most detailed part, leaving me with a lumpy mass of fish belly, the scales lacking definition, like an ancient relic in a second-rate museum. These bigger fish come prepackaged in single-serve boxes or in square plastic pouches at gas stations, the kind where the top is so solidly welded to itself that when you try to pull it apart, you get a gaping maw in the front.

The rarer and better Swedish Fish are tinier, firmer, rendered in greater detail. I always tell people this and they never know what I'm talking about. The smaller ones are a more saturated red, I insist, and more satisfying to bite. I Chicken Little my way around, concerned that people are missing out, trying to find someone who understands me. If I'm wrong, I hope this is at least a manifestation of the Mandela effect— a phenomenon where masses of people hold false memories for things that never happened or existed. But I've yet to find anyone living in this same dream.

The littler ones, whether in this quantum timeline or another, are infinitely superior in flavor, and far cuter. Cherry gummies, right? Nope. Not cherry but lingonberry, a tartish cousin of cranberry that grows from an appropriately Scandinavian evergreen shrub. (Shout-out here to my friend Isaac, who thought it was Loganberry, named for some guy named Logan.) Not gummies but starch jellies—meaning they contain no gelatin, no trace of hoof or bone, and are therefore vegan. Funny how a ubiquitous thing can be almost universally misunderstood on its most basic level. How much knowledge, and how much memory, we hold without realizing it's totally flawed. We are always operating by skewed coordinates, whether we know it or not.

These small ones are best in bulk, at the last few places where you can buy penny candy. When I was little, I got them at the Magic Lantern, a movie theater that had stood in our town since the 1920s. It was, for some reason, on the

second floor, and a real red carpet flowed up the steep stairs beneath a shining brass handrail. In the upper hallway, there was a player piano that really played, and the penny candy counter had some candy that really was a penny, although the bigger stuff—Squirrel Nut Zippers, Bulls-Eyes—could be two or three cents each. A person would scoop your candies for you, plunging a metal trowel into each heavy glass jar, and hand them to you in a plastic bag. Maybe he'd jauntily twirl it shut as he sailed it over the counter and down to your little waiting hand. I loved the Magic Lantern completely, for all these things and every other thing about it—the flocked wallpaper, the tasseled velvet drapes along the walls and on either side of the screen, the framed posters of stars from the black-and-white era, their eyebrows penciled on just like my grandmother's. It smelled like dust, and buttered popcorn, with the best fake butter, served in red-striped paper buckets. The Magic Lantern was a time machine, a crossroads between the future and the past: I watched movies set in gleaming cities and imagined myself grown up and striding down those crowded sidewalks, busy and glamorous, while cozy on the worn plush seats of that ancient theater. Mom was always happy at the movies, and I was, too, and we always felt clever when we went to weekend matinees to hide awhile from the heat, escaping summer for an artificial fall. When I launched my memoir in my hometown of Bridgton, the town's small bookstore rented out the Magic Lantern for the occasion, and I realized I had become the future self I'd dreamed of in the projector's flickering light.

The smaller Swedish Fish do legitimately taste better, but it's their smallness, not their flavor, that makes them special. Poet and critic Susan Stewart writes of the "capacity of the miniature to create an 'other' time, a type of transcendent time which negates change and the flux of lived reality," and so the tiniest gummy fish not only take me back to childhood but suspend me there, in a bright, unchanging orb of simple happiness. Science has even described how our perception of time is affected by spatial dimensions. When researchers asked people to imagine themselves performing various activities while peering into a 1:12 scale model environment, and then asked them when they felt thirty minutes had passed, they discovered that the participants experienced half an hour in one-twelfth the time: two and a half "real-world" minutes. For the participants, time had slowed down dramatically: at that scale, thirty real minutes would have felt like six hours.

Just as miniature environments slow down time, images on the big screen speed it up. When we immerse ourselves in a larger-than-life story on a glowing theater screen, we escape the passing hours of our own lives, compressed and forgotten. (Think of stumbling out into an evening after a long matinee, the shock of disappeared light.) Under the colossal shining faces projected by and projecting our desire, we are moved through the predetermined time of a story we cannot pause or rewind, locked in intimate darkness with strangers we may never see again. Light coming from behind and above us, speakers on either side of us, we're literally surrounded by the story. We are moved as we sit still. We ride time, flashing forward and back, skipping through montages, considering a woman's teary face for long, aching seconds, barely noticing that our perspective is determined by the camera's decisions. These tiny fish sacraments allow us to enter Stewart's "infinite time of reverie," the effects of the tiny and the gigantic disorienting us so that we're suspended in a swirling present, the gaze and the body conspiring to finally obliterate daily clock time.

When I think of eating Swedish Fish at the Magic Lantern, I remember Mom and me watching *Interview with the Vampire,* featuring a twelve-year-old Kirsten Dunst. Kirsten and I were exactly the same age, blond and round-faced. In that role, she had the serious air I occasionally had, that adults would praise as precocious, that would eventually assure them I was "well adjusted"—our personalities escaping the expectations of our age. A year later, Mom would be gone and I would fly to a faraway state to live with an aunt I barely knew, and the flight attendant would be one of the first of many people, over the next ten years or so, to tell me I looked like Dunst. Even under those circumstances, it pleased me to resemble a movie star, the face I had seen shining so large above me, the face of someone who already had greater access to the world than I could yet dream of, the face of a character who would live forever and never leave anyone behind.

I remember all this, but memory is creative and cannot always be trusted. "Remember" is a verb. My mind has bent time to make all this happen: *Interview with the Vampire* didn't come out until six months after Mom died. If I ate Swedish Fish while watching it, it was at some corporate theater in a Texas mall, not the Magic Lantern, and they were likely the big, chewy ones, out of a box. The flight I remember was probably the next summer, on my way back to Maine to visit relatives, on my way back to a haunted land. I'm surprised to discover these distortions, but not very. This isn't the only movie that I've imagined watching with Mom but never could have: in the few years after her death, it was easy to bring her consciousness with me into a story in the dark. I still experienced everything not only through my own perception, but through my idea of hers. Then, afterward, I would forget that she had existed only within me, hadn't been sitting there beside me, munching individual pops of corn with clean fingers. For years I would replay the memory of sitting on our couch with her while watching *Bound,* the slick Wachowski lesbian neo-noir, staring rapt at the screen while trying to feel whether she could feel how much I enjoyed it, and how that made her feel, but that movie came out more than two years after she died. And of course *Interview* stayed with me. Dunst's character, Claudia, is an orphan—her mother dead, her father unmentioned—when Lestat finds and transforms her into the undead. She becomes enraged when she understands that she is doomed to remain a twelve-year-old orphan for eternity, excruciatingly trapped outside the forward march of time. When Claudia screams "I had a mother once!" she understands that love, mortality, and time are inextricably bound.

I wish I could take that little vampire to a movie, give her some tiny sweet fish, and for a little while take her mind off everything she'd lost, show her that moving through time was a skill that could be learned like anything else, that somehow she'd find her own ways to get it moving again.

On Twizzlers Filled Bites, Strawberry

These come in a free-range bag: you can dive your hand in and pull them out without doing any further unwrapping. The bag has a zipper—which is useful, because even I took three sessions to finish. They're satisfying little nuggets, each about half an inch long, and the texture is finer and softer than regular Twizzlers, reminiscent of all the soft plastic toys you chewed on as a kid. They retain the outer texture of the twist, a raised channel that's, again, more finely made than the original. By which I mean thinner, with a higher resolution. They feel almost 3D printed. The strawberry flavor is good, not mind-bending but adequate, like the red of a red crayon.

Sophie, my partner Preston's ex-girlfriend, gave these to me when we visited her little beachside town a year or so after the complications of distance and Covid ended their romantic relationship. We're polyamorous, so she and I were both dating him back then, in the days when he lived there for a writing residency. In poly parlance, that made us "metamours"—dating the same person but not dating each other. When Preston and I arrived for this visit, we were all friends once more. Sophie left my Bites on top of a stack of neatly folded white towels in our room. He received a tub of unsalted nuts. This shows that she knows us both. We met up with her at the beach soon after we arrived, snacks in tow, and hung out with her big family.

The inside is smushy, a soft filling. More vulnerable than the finely made outside might indicate (like Sophie herself). It's strange to think of cooking in any traditional sense of the word here, but it's as though the inside is less cooked. Although the Bites are open-ended, perhaps made in one long tube and then cut (not sealed), they hold up to beach heat, don't melt or goo out. Still, when you bite them, you can feel the smoothness inside, squishing out onto your gums.

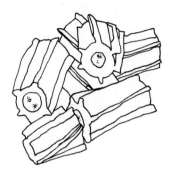

I wouldn't have thought I would support any sort of Twizzlers innovation, but this is a good one. I wouldn't have thought Sophie and I would still have friendship and love between us, but we do. Neat on the outside, sweeter and messier inside.

Hard Reds

On Cinnamon Hearts

A tiny rain of spiky heat, bright red, with subtle indentations at the heart top. Each about the size of a pinkie nail, with a thick, glossy coat of shine, sometimes decorating cupcakes, thrown softly down into thick swirls of buttercream, extra fancy points for the baker. More often you pour them from a box into your hand, or your mouth, or scatter them on your desk, admiring their shape, how each one balances on a little convex spot on its side, seeming almost to float. Eat a single one and it's almost an itch on the tongue, a spark of sugary herbal heat. Throw in a little handful and your mouth floods, protecting its own soft tissues, drawing out and melting down a flavor just this side of troublesome.

Cinnamon hearts arrived at Valentine's, but I didn't see them every year. They came in loose bags like chocolate chips, or in tiny boxes that themselves were valentines, with *To:* and *From:* lines on the side. To address them, you had to pinch the box in place with one hand while pressing the other firmly to the table, trying to make your handwriting look nice.

Back then, in childhood, it was okay to declare love for multiple people at a time. I guess I never unlearned that.

The best part of cinnamon hearts is the name, the staccato rhythm of "cinn-a-mon" ending in the sure foot plant of "hearts," like a practiced hopscotch run. Pigtail bounce and turn, do it again. Cinn-a-mon hearts, sure and crisp, like the crush I had on my classmate Jacob Huntress, year after elementary school year. He was blond like me, with freckled cheeks like me but athletic and reliably sunny. I loved him secretly each year from first grade through fifth, in an unhurried way, thinking that we were destined to be married. When Mom drove me to my grandmother's, we'd pass Jacob's grandparents' house by the golf course—or at least I thought it was their house, held this idea in the unspoken, unexamined way of children—and each time I imagined standing with Jacob under their arched white trellis, next to their little man-made pond.

The picture was full, and serene: maple leaves casting dappled light on us from high above, rows and rows of family and friends smiling gently at us from bright white folding chairs. Wrapped in heavy white satin, I'd cry, shoulders shaking under floating tulle, and he'd give me the wide, easy smile from his third-grade class portrait, shoulders tuxedo solid, broad and inviting. I'd be the sharp cinnamon and he the sugar, the unbothered, the placid, and I'd borrow calm from him, from his comfortable white-haired grandparents, his mother with the thickening middle. He had the brightest blue eyes. But at school we hardly ever spoke—while he ran the soccer field, I sat leaning against the chain link under the trees, reading novels or listening to David Bowie captured from the radio on a Maxell cassette, during hours of lying on my scratchy carpet hovering near the Record button, waiting for "Jean Genie." He's probably golfing right now.

Now I think the crush had less to do with the person and more to do with "Jacob Huntress": first name like something to savor, the *J* a tear of teeth, the hard *c* gently tapping the deep palate, the *b* a tiny soft kiss before parting; last name summoning androgynous Diana—a strong woman striding the woods, face up to the light in bright clearings, leaping like a stag along dark, twisting trails, just as I imagined myself in my wanderings behind our house on weekends, the idea of romance always competing with my first love, solitude.

Words and the pleasures they name have always been closely related for me. Did I love the boy or his name? Do I actually love cinnamon or just the symbol, the practice of eating one heart after another, the reckless insistence on loving until it's all gone?

On Starlight Mints

Portable disks of candy cane, perfect for those of us who don't like to get our hands sticky. Hold each end of the wrapper between thumb and forefinger and pull, watching it spin open.

Just think: once you had tiny hands, and someone taught you to do this. The sound is delicious, the crackle of distant fireworks, the gold ones that rain down like stars.

The mint itself is a bit dangerous, like the curved cane it resembles. Smooth at first, it reveals a texture once it melts, your saliva carving caverns into it like dissolved limestone, the red melting faster than the white. The edges of these gorges are sharp and will slash the eager animal of your tongue. The soft skin of the inside of your cheek is especially vulnerable; a greedy suck will slice you. So eat these with delicacy, then violence: bite before the razor appears in your mouth.

On Tootsie Pops

An über-candy, the psychic template for American lollipops. A serious classic, unstoppable, good fresh and good old and good even after having melted in the car, when you have to pull the wrapper off as best you can, then suck until you can remove the last bits of paper, squinting as sunshine strobes through the trees as your mother drives you home from a doctor's appointment.

This pop was a two-step pleasure. First, the hard candy outside—in cherry or raspberry or slightly disappointing orange, or the rarer grape or chocolate—then the chewy chocolate inside. Was the hard carapace just a prelude or an event unto itself? They were named, after all, for what was inside. The candy's slogan presented this dilemma as an urgent modern mystery: "How many licks does it take to get to the center of a Tootsie Pop?" Not a catchy sentence, but still a fun game. In the cartoon ads, a bland little boy took his query to a succession of animals, most memorably an owl, who would try to answer the question—"Wah-unn, two-hooo!, tha-reee"—and then fail, crunching into the candy sphere with his beak as desire overtook him. He wore glasses, his big blue eyeballs filling the round frames, and he was crowned with a mortarboard. He was a professor, a physicist of candy, and even he couldn't resist messing up the experiment. How many licks? Well, a serious voice would intone, "The world may never know." Watching this ad, I and many other thousands of children resolved to find out, to patiently melt down that outside shell in a manner calculable and recorded. Surely we could crack the mysteries that confounded adults and cartoon animals. It seemed a simple task, to lick without biting, to enjoy one pleasure while waiting for another.

It was impossible. I always bit, impatient for the Tootsie Roll nugget inside. That was the part that really made your mouth water, even if it was mostly in response to the sudden shift in texture, the center so yielding and immediately rewarding.

The hard-candy outside would shatter into tiny pieces, which melted instantly like snowflakes on the tongue. It was a pleasurable failure, a queer sensation. There were choices to be made, the ego and the id in a delicate dance, but there was wisdom to giving in to desire. As the challenge had been presented, so, too, had the joy of defeat—Mr. Owl was played, after all, by Paul Winchell, also the original voice of Tigger, that purveyor of delightful chaos.

I still crunch into a Tootsie Pop before its hard-candy shell has entirely faded away. This alters my usual rhythm of candy eating, which is characterized by savoring—patient licks, gentle melting, doling out individual pieces to make the experience last as long as possible. What I cannot do is delay the start: if there's candy in the house, it's monumentally difficult for me not to eat it. It magnetizes my attention. In the presence of candy, there is no neutral state. There is eating or distraction.

I have always wondered how I would fare (as a child and, if we're being honest, today) in the infamous Stanford marshmallow experiment, in which researchers imprisoned kids in a bare room with a single marshmallow and told them that if they waited fifteen minutes to eat it, they would earn a second one. Setting aside the question of how this torture got IRB approval, I want to state that marshmallows are one of the least exciting possible candies with which to run this experiment. (Are they even candies? Really more of an ingredient.) But I get it: they are uniform in shape, plain white, pretty purely just sugar, and resistant to vagaries of personal taste and allergy. Unless you're vegan. Unless you have issues with corn syrup. (Helen Betya Rubinstein, in her excellent essay "On Not Eating the Marshmallow," points out that this study could no longer be run at the preschool where it originated, given parental food anxieties.) They tested the kids in the 1970s, then tracked their life success, as measured by all the boring, typical American markers—test performance, thinness, coolness under pressure. The initial results were published in *Science* in 1989, when I was eight, and that paper and all later follow-ups asserted the value of delayed gratification: Kids who were able to wait for that second marshmallow had higher SAT scores. They had lower BMIs, were more popular. They were less likely to get divorced. We don't know if they were kinder, more creative, more likely to feel their lives had purpose.

It's true that delaying gratification has benefits: if you focus enough to do your homework before going outside to play, day after day, the system will reward you. Or so we thought. Researchers at NYU and UC Irvine recently ran the marshmallow test again, this time with a larger, more diverse group of kids. When the results were adjusted for household income and other factors of privilege, the ability to wait for the second treat had a limited effect on "success." Poor kids who exerted self-control did no better in life than those who didn't, and the same went for the rich kids. It was—surprise—the groups' relative poverty or affluence that made the real difference.

So Mr. Owl was right to chomp, and I was foolish to think myself wiser than a professorial raptor. The recent study even found that affluent kids were better able to wait for that second marshmallow, proving once more that abundance replicates itself. Not only did their backgrounds set them up for high test scores, but their comfort in the world got them more candy in laboratory settings. This aligns with other research that shows that those who struggle financially are more likely to avail themselves of short-term rewards, even those they can't technically afford, and that poor parents are more likely to give in when their kids ask for sugar.

What the marshmallow experiment, in both its iterations, failed to measure was the children's enjoyment of the marshmallows. This seems an egregious oversight, for what are all those personal and professional accomplishments worth if our path to attaining them is dull? Numerous studies suggest that effort and anticipation increase happiness and enjoyment. (My favorite is "Waiting for Merlot: Anticipatory Consumption of Experiential and Material Purchases.") But still, I wonder: was the sugar more delicious for the children who waited—made sweeter not just by the neurological processes of anticipation and reward but by being evidence of that sweetest thing, a fulfilled promise—or for the children who plunged forward and ate the first marshmallow immediately, sharpening their enjoyment with a transgressive edge?

There's a danger in delaying our gratifications indefinitely. Much has been made of the paradoxical decisions that those who bear the crushing weight of scarcity sometimes make— stories about poor parents buying their kids PlayStations when they can't afford organic vegetables, or lottery tickets as a "poverty tax," always get traction. We're eager to punish those who would seek excess or joy before attending to basic needs, while ignoring how difficult or impossible it might be to ever cover those bills. How long should people wait to live? How big should people be allowed to dream? Less attention has been paid to those who, raised in poverty, obsessively conserve money and resources, who, after having pulled themselves out of precarity, still feel unsafe, feel intense guilt about small indulgences, who, when they receive that second marsh-mallow, still sit staring, eating neither of them, who are given a Tootsie Pop at the bank and then carry it in their pocket, saving it for someday, a someday they never allow themselves, never recognize, until it's sticky and covered in lint.

The marshmallow kids who could imagine the two-marshmallow future so vividly that it became more real than the fragrant, glowing single marshmallow before them were the ones who could hold out. They had hope that the researcher would return—they had learned that adults kept promises. Their parents had rarely picked them up late due to car trouble, had rarely failed to buy them a promised gift because the money ran out. The kids who ate the first marsh-mallow, the thinking goes, had been let down too many times to believe that the second one would appear.

But maybe those kids felt hope, too. Maybe they indulged because they thought there might be more lab days in the future; bought the PlayStation because, sure, they couldn't afford it now, but things were bound to improve any minute; bit into the Tootsie Pop because there would be countless other chances to run the experiment and beat Mr. Owl.

Struggle is unbearable without hope, and hope, for kids, takes the form of imagination, of magic. Hidden on certain rare Tootsie Pop wrappers, we learned, was a spell: a boy in a headdress drawing an arrow across a bow, pointed at a star. (Tootsie Roll Industries, I think you can retire the magical Native American trope now, as several Indigenous groups have asked you to.) You could save these special wrappers and redeem them for . . . toys? Free candy? A million dollars? It was never clear. But supposedly, if you handed the wrapper to a benevolent grocery store clerk you would receive a prize, and then all daily magic would be reinforced. I've since learned that this character is no rarer than any other image on the Tootsie Pop toile wrapper, and of course the whole thing was an urban legend. But I saved them, never tried to redeem them. I kept them in a little box with other treasures, signs that I was lucky, that Mom and I were, that maybe someday our weekly lottery tickets would erase all our worries and we would have everything we wanted, whenever we wanted it. In the meantime, Mom let me eat as much candy as I pleased.

On Luden's Wild Cherry

A candy, yes. The ingredients: pectin (candy), ascorbic and citric acid (candy), corn syrup, and sucrose (candy, candy). Not one herb or extract or tincture. If you had a halfway decent childhood, your mom kept these around for your recurrent kiddo colds. They came in a white box with neat, sharp corners, about two-thirds the size of the Junior Mints box. This was wrapped in cellophane, which kept the drops fresh while also giving them a medicinal air, accessorized with a bright red pull strip exactly like the one on Marlboro packs. My mouth waters just thinking of pulling that strip.

Luden's were delicious, a bright red cherry flavor, a flavor like seeing your friend's face again after weeks apart. A happy flavor that made you almost glad you were sick. The lozenges themselves were pretty small, kid-size rectangles with rounded corners, "Luden's" embossed on each one between emphatic lines above and below, which you melted down and smoothed as you ate them. Unlike most items marketed as hard candy, they weren't shiny, had instead a sort of dull, old-fashioned-

looking matte finish, probably unchanged since their creation in 1879.

Is it too sentimental to say that the medicine you were getting was your mom's love? Each drop meant to soothe not just your throat but your heart? Mine brought them out only when I was sick. We wrote, together, the story that they were medicine. Most of the time it was just the two of us: we could decide what anything meant in our house.

On Strawberry Hard Candy in the Strawberry Wrapper

Strawberry on strawberry, an inception candy. *Strawberry!* these proclaim, their shiny metallic red-and-green wrappers a cybernetic interpretation of the fruit, the end point of a flower's life cycle transposed into Trapper Keeper aesthetics. They're a twist-wrapper situation, but twisted on only one end, so there's a red, seed-spotted butt topped by a bright green flourish of foil, mimicking leaves. The transition is a zigzag of green on red, drawn with Seussian enthusiasm. The shape is pineapple, but no matter.

Sometimes "Brach's" is printed on them, in the boldly

clashing purple of the company name, which is pure obnoxiousness, akin to those subscription cards that rain down when you're trying to read a magazine to which you've already subscribed. Why must I be pelted with advertisements for the very thing I'm currently enjoying? I've already done what you want, I've already given you my money, leave me alone.

Inside is a simple oval lozenge, nicely bright red, like a Luden's with no medical pretensions. It's another hard candy with no shine, all shine duties taken up by the wrapper. It has a slight matte texture, and if your mouth is dry it can even briefly stick there on your tongue. But then your own liquid will rush in, salivary glands perhaps kicking in that painful, aching way, eager to break it down. The hard candy experience is lovely, solid, of dependable texture and speed, and then you get to what you forgot was the main event: a molten strawberry center. Strawberry on strawberry on strawberry! Was there ever a candy more ecstatic, more insistent on its own essence?

The molten center has a gel texture, and it comes out just when the hard candy exterior is starting to get sharp. So it's a candy with its own lube. After the seductive call of the shiny wrapper, this baby isn't going to leave you unprepared, is going to smooth the way through the whole act.

Never mind that I'm sexualizing a candy that isn't so much crafted by a company as it is spontaneously sprung from the bottoms of grandmothers' purses. Grandmothers have sex lives, too.

On Atomic FireBalls

"Cinnamon," a word topped with gentle hills, a word signaling sepia-toned spice in a burlap sack on a verdant mountainside, is completely inappropriate to the experience of FireBalls, although cinnamon is what they are. These are fire-engine red, half-inch spheres that will burn your tongue if you leave them in one spot too long. As you suck on one, you can feel the cloud of cinnamon fumes around you, an aura that brushes your face and reaches out into the void. Will it attract or repel? Hard to tell. The candy itself is a complex experience—painful, something to be suffered through, but pleasurable, too: the ultra-concentrated spice spiked with capsaicin, the chemical that makes peppers burn, but counterbalanced by sugar, all bound by some dense material that makes the ball last and last, perhaps some kind of guar

gum or another such hard-to-pronounce ingredient I've read off candy wrappers while idly tasting.

These are technically discontinued, but you can still find them through a few internet shops. There are trends in candy, and cinnamon seems to have faded into the background. (Here let's pause for a moment to mourn Cinnaburst gum.)

It was fun to give a FireBall to someone on the playground, either telling them or just letting them believe it was cherry-flavored. They'd pop it in their mouth, then their face would scrunch. "Argh," they'd say, and you'd laugh, and they'd either spit it out right away or flail their hands and arms, puckering and sucking their way through it, because it was still candy, after all, and candy on the playground was an extra good thing. It meant that you or someone else had planned ahead, had waited and resisted, so that you could have sugar and swing sets and blazing green grass all together, the teacher on the other side of the field and not motivated, outside, to tell you that you couldn't have it if you hadn't brought enough for everyone. You could share with just one person, an intimate exchange, even if the sharing included laughing at them, even if it taught them that sometimes generosity is suspect.

On Drugstore Candy Canes

You know the ones—they come in a thin cardboard tray, lying on their backs in a row, each nested into its own slot, the short ends curled up like the paws of a puppy on its back. They're protected by a screen of clear plastic, and it's satisfying to break it when you get home, by stretch-poking it with your finger or, if you want to get fancy about it, slicing through it with a knife or scissors. It's the crème brûlée–top moment. The beginning of Christmas. Hang half on the tree and put the other half on your desk, to wait there for idle moments, when you peel one open and stick it into your slack mouth, salivating and sucking over spreadsheets or tax returns or, if you're lucky, something creative, maybe essays about candy.

Which end you stick in your mouth is an existential question, one that reveals what sort of person you are. Most unwrap the plastic from the long end and start there, using the curve as a handle, which I suppose reflects the design of the thing, form following function. But this convenience belies forethought: at the end, you have an awkward turn of hard candy, a U shape that doesn't fit in the mouth fully. That bend is also too small to put one arm of the thing into your mouth; the other will poke your outer cheek. At best, you can bite it in half, a risky proposition given its freshness, its lack of meltdown—it will inevitably shatter all over your desk or counter or table. In recent years, I've finally started turning my candy cane around, eating the curve first, retaining the long stick end for a handle. Like when we all learned, seemingly at once, that monkeys eat bananas by peeling them from the pinched end and using the stem for a handle, instead of the other way around, like most humans do. Once we realized this, we felt stupid. For one flash moment, we understood that we were the inferior, dumber species. It was, of course, a moment we immediately forgot. You'd think climate change would keep us ever cognizant of this fact. You'd think by now we'd be praying to the whales deep in the water, we'd be collecting the finest seeds for the birds we have remaining. But no.

Candy canes on trees dress up death, perhaps human-kind's best skill. How festive! One more tree cut down, and, well, it was destined to be cut down, right? That's why we put it there.

Still, I have no plans to opt out. I loathe a fake Christmas tree, judge each owner as a killjoy who shouldn't bother with a tree at all. Without the fresh spruce smell, amplified by the waft of peppermint from the stick below your nose, what's the point? And is a fake tree so much better, environmentally? I think of the petroleum used to make the plastic needles, like that used to make fake leather, and the cellophane on candy cane packages, and then I think of the fields and fertilizer of the tree farms, my own meat-eating, cows and methane, Greta Thunberg shaking her blond head at me in my own head. Hopeless. Baby Jesus is not coming to save us from this one. We've known since at least 1979.

We're not fixing this anytime soon. If we attend to our small, flawed joys in the meantime, is that complacency? I set out to celebrate a celebration, a dozen sticks of sugar in a cheery box, all striped red and white, flavored with an oil from a leaf. When did we first learn that this lovely smell could be taken into our bodies, how did we know it wouldn't kill us? Have you ever taken a leaf of peppermint between your teeth? It's divine. Slightly furry. You can feel the water in its cells if you bite, the rain that reached it, quiet of a gray afternoon. I think of the low mountains of my birth home, where we could pick these leaves, where we watched for the shine of poison ivy, where blueberries grew so abundantly you could smell them as you approached. The paper bark of birch trees, ash trunks giving way beneath the brushing of your fingertips, and the pines, of course, rising to the sky, unclimbable trunks branchless until twenty feet up, alternating between blocking and bestowing light. To take a candy cane onto a snowy trail, later in the year, was to remember the plant now buried, destined to return with the spring.

On Life Savers

A Life Saver is a tiny O of hard candy, neatly stacked in a row in a paper-and-foil sleeve, jewel-toned, waiting for the precise moment you need it. What a name for a candy: You're drowning in your day, stressors and demands swamping you. You need a break, a moment to yourself. This is a common narrative in candy advertisements aimed at adults: *Take a moment. Have some pleasure.* But there's melancholy here. The pleasure isn't for itself, not abundance or joy as its own end. It accrues its value only in opposition to suffering or boredom. The delight has pain as its precondition, and despite the fact that one could argue this is always the case—we cannot feel the warmth of happiness without first standing in the cold rain of melancholy, etc., etc.—it's a lot to put on a candy. Life Saver: sugar the only thing standing between you and world-ending despair. And so a Life Saver keeps you afloat, keeps you, maybe, from getting out of the water that threatens to pull you down. Advertising as the part of the capitalist machine that keeps us all just content enough to keep swimming.

Yes, of course: sometimes, for me, sugar has saved the day. But it's too much to ask of a little loop of sugar and flavor; it's a lot to promise, so explicitly.

Red, as usual, is my favorite flavor. A red Life Saver is an idea of a ripe, supple cherry condensed and frozen into an industrial ring of hard sugar, divorced from any imaginings of orchards, whisperings of wind-tousled leaves, the gentle murmurs of bees. I grew up eating Life Savers on Maine lakes—literally on, sitting in the bottoms of canoes, held just below the waterline—and in fields cleared from thick woods, pushing aside tall grasses as I cut across from one tree-shaded area to another. I ate them in cars winding through forests, one hand out the window to cup the rushing air. There was often this tension between the industrial, the nationally marketed, and that slow small-town rhythm.

The TV products never delivered the promised shiny life, too much of it cast against the streets and glass of faraway cities. Still, I mixed silver lamé shoes and blue lipstick with my woodsy flannels, like any other nineties kid, even if there were few to see this cyber-influenced style. I rolled my eyes at goths in careful white face paint, sitting on green town squares and romanticizing death, but my disdain covered my envy, my respect for their boldness. Still, I wouldn't have wanted to make my identity dependent on getting my aunt to drive me the forty-five minutes to the nearest town with a mall and a Spencer's and a Hot Topic.

But I had to wear something, and the better things were from that same mall. And unless your small town houses a confectioner's, your candy will be mass-produced, shiny, glossy, caught in the machine of desire manipulation that is the US economy. Pleasure is never pure.

Life Savers, in their bright fruit flavors, in their pop ubiquity, should be a happy symbol. Clarence Crane originally produced them in 1912 as a "summer candy," after all—a treat that wouldn't melt in the heat, that would save you from the disappointment of ruined chocolate bars. But now I'm remembering: he was the father of the poet Hart Crane, who threw himself, fatally, into the arms of the sea. After I left the lakes for the cities, where I dressed with an awareness of audience, joining an ongoing visual conversation—where I worked, for a time, in a tall glass tower where I often cried in the bathroom— I was constantly in need of a lifesaver and found it in the company of fellow queer writers, for whom Crane and all the other tragic twentieth-century gay poets were saints. *Did you know*, we'd say to one another, leaning over sticky bar tables in the dark, *that his father invented the Life Saver?* We'd picture the literal, original object, white and red, floating away on a cold ocean, the water undisturbed, Hart sinking below. Then we'd sit back quietly in the booth, savoring that dark irony and hoping our careers turned out better.

Green

On Andes Mints

n my childhood, Andes mints on the bill tray meant you were at a fancy restaurant. They were class itself, their metallic paper wrapper shining green like amped-up money. The fact that you had only one to savor made you sophisticated, and the sharply defined edges of the chocolate added to their rarefied air. The logo, embossed on each piece, is a stylized mountain range with "Andes" in the foreground, textured horizontal lines in the background, a design that strikes me as a bit midcentury modern, now that I know they debuted in 1950. Andes at a restaurant connected us to the outside world, rituals of taste that I would eagerly absorb, that were wrapped up in my desire to go to college, to become a writer, to live in a city, to vacation on tropical islands—to have the money and leisure to do all of this, all these things that my mother never got to do, that almost no one in my family did or has done, except for my aunt Glenice.

Andes and all they represented were the reason I forgave Glenice the year she got irritated with her sister Carol for not having a proper bread knife to cut the fine loaf Glenice had

brought for Thanksgiving. Glenice had long lived in Boston, while Carol never left Maine. Most in the family took Carol's side: Glenice was being "snotty" and "had a tone" when she asked about the knife she should have known wasn't there, in a solidly Pepperidge Farm house. I could see that her irritation was transmuted sadness, that she had only wanted to share something special, something that represented her current life, the one no one but Mom and I had ever visited. Everyone else expected her to return to the woods to see them, because, they said, they couldn't handle the traffic and wouldn't dream of taking a bus down there, no matter how comfortable. All those years and almost no one had seen her apartment— a beautiful space with capacious reading chairs and deep-pile carpets that absorbed every footstep and suncatchers hanging in the windows, a sanctuary she had carefully built herself over years of working as a dental assistant. She wanted her siblings to appreciate this small, golden loaf, at least, but if you cut crusty bread with a smooth-edged knife, the pieces come out smushed, disappointing. The outer shell shatters all over the counter. Glenice had wanted to nicely present this thing that represented her, the life she had built far from home. She wasn't trying to make a mess.

Watching this all unfold in my teens, I resolved to be a person who had the knowledge to enjoy fine things and the generosity to share them. It was partially an impulse to upward mobility, but not totally; it was also about curiosity and a sense of adventure, the reasons Mom was excited to visit Glenice in the city. She liked going to museums and trying Thai food and riding the T, where once we saw a man standing calmly with a huge snake wrapped around his shoulders. By the time of the bread incident, Mom was gone and I was the only one left to take Glenice's side, continuing my trajectory out into the world, which we both wished didn't involve a rejection of where we came from, a rejection sometimes foisted on us by others. These days, Preston, raised in much more comfortable circumstances, marvels at my knowledge of fabrics and materials and foods, attempting to stump me while shopping or eating out. *That's raw silk; I can smell it. Langoustines are shellfish. Churchill's hat, in that old photo, is likely astrakhan.*

But fanciness is contextual. Andes mints at home were more intimate. We'd get them most often at Christmastime, their green-striped edge perfect for the season. We would nibble them delicately on the couch while watching *Seinfeld,* my first window onto the glories and absurdities of New York City life. Grief is enormous, but it is also made of small, sharp pains, and one of these is that Mom would never visit me when I lived uptown, a block away from Tom's Restaurant, whose exterior serves as the diner where Jerry and his friends gather. I would love to have stood on that corner, embarrassed while Mom insisted on taking a picture.

Andes come neatly lined up on their sides in a cushioned box and slide out like business cards. They have a wonderfully snappy consistency, which you can increase by putting them in the freezer, where the chocolate stands up to the cold, only hardening, not going brittle or white. The mint is a distinct, pale green layer, not blended in, and the visual cue allows you to better taste it, just as green mint chocolate chip ice cream is better than white, however inorganic the coloring might be. The size of an Andes is just right, a long rectangle proportioned to the tongue.

Mom loved these, as she loved all sweet mints, and I can see her sitting on our couch in her bright blue terry-cloth robe, reaching for another one with a barely perceptible air of mischief, both of us laughing as Kramer slides into the apartment once again. I never had any self-control and would strain to limit myself to one row of Andes per day, so she'd have a chance of having some. Like most mothers, she constantly sacrificed her own small pleasures so I could have more. While I dreamed myself onto the sidewalk below Jerry's fire escape, she knew she would remain among the trees, a home base for me to return to. Now I hope she occasionally hid her own box of Andes somewhere, to enjoy in secret. She would never have the chance to move away from her hometown, she would never start that community college degree, she would never leave the factory where she hand-sewed leather shoes, paid by the unit. But she had her pleasures, and her imagination and openness, and the occasional visit to Boston, to feed them, and I have my love and grief, and my gratitude to Glenice, the one family member who helped her experience more of the world, in the time that she had.

On Green Apple Jolly Ranchers

These are angling golden sunlight on after-school trips—in my case, band or math team. (I have always been very cool.) One sort of day ending and another beginning, and everyone's vibration strengthened, whether low or high. The rambunctious kids are rambunctioning, the quieter kids are sitting with books in the middle and front of the bus. I was most likely to be reading, or talking with a friend or two. Everyone was likely, in those years of the nineties, to be eating a green apple Jolly Rancher. Everyone but me.

Ten or so minutes into the ride, I'd hear it—the staticky crackle of a wrapper, followed by a scent tendril of sugar and synthetic green flavor, then the solid pop of something hitting the inside of someone's molars. A kissy sucking noise, and then the full bloom of the thing would release, a near-violent aroma of sugar and sweet and tart, more smell than made sense, more molecules of scent than seemed possible from such a small nugget, perfuming and then filling the bus, that tinny enclosed space, crowding the oxygen and tinting it green. I'd be gossiping with a friend and then suddenly the scent was all I could think about, threading up through my nostrils and into my brain, jamming my networks. Fucking Jolly Ranchers, once again.

I'd tried this flavor and it was fine, okay, it was a hard candy, it was extra super hard, it's true, so hard you had to wonder what else was in it, because sugar and flavor alone couldn't be so hard, could it? So impermeable to saliva and time. Surely there was some other concretious binding agent? It lasted and lasted, which was fine for the eating, fine when

you had one, but hell when you were merely near one, stuck on a sickeningly wobbling bus, the floors coated in who knew what, stickiness you hadn't noticed before someone twisted open that wrapper and availed themselves of this pleasure, the sort of pleasure that, when nearby but not shared and not requested, only causes you to feel sick, like that of a subway masturbator. Sure, that person's actions over there, having nothing to do with you, merely in your line of sight, shouldn't bother you, in the abstract. But you can't block it out—it's happening so intensely, so near, its invisible vectors of enjoyment bank-shotting off the wall and onto you.

And smell—smell you can't get away from. You can't direct your line of smell. A green apple Jolly Rancher on a bus was an assault, uncalled for, inescapable. (Green apple was the worst flavor, a synthetic mockery of apples, offensively tangy, but watermelon, too, was unbearable, an arrogant overshot approximation of summer days and fruit meat. There was no good version of this thing.) I'd open my window to the frosty winter wind, ignoring the pleas of the person behind me, the admonishment of the driver. I'd imagine sticking my head out like a dog, cold wind numbing my teeth and, more importantly, my nose. Fucking Jolly Ranchers, they were endless, the eater mindlessly sucking and talking, the smell finally making me truly nauseated. But there was no escape. The irritating bodily connections of youth—all the humid shared beds of sleepovers, the musty pinnies of group games in gym class, the occasional period leak before you'd learned your rhythms, your morphing body on display with all the others—were intimacies that you often had no choice but to accept.

So, although they were the most condensed, longest-lasting little log of sugar you could find, I hated these things. I begged people not to eat them in enclosed spaces, but of course, that's what they were made for. To pass the time, to bring pleasure to waiting, to the trip from one place to another, one state to another. Like youth itself, sometimes that transition was enjoyable, and sometimes you just had to wait it out.

On Chinese Candy My Friend Liz Brings Me

Liz gets these tiny hard candy balls from her brother in San Francisco and brings them to me infrequently enough to surprise me each time she pulls them from her bag. They have a delicate, strangely buttery flavor, citrus plus something more savory, herbal, like nothing else we've ever tasted. They are nothing short of mesmerizing, each one such a complex experience you need only a few to feel sated. They are the only candy that I can actually keep in my house for longer than a day.

In truth, it's only partly their interesting flavor that keeps me from wiping these candies out immediately. Mostly it's that I treasure them, as I treasure Liz and our monthlyish coffee hangouts. We'll pick a Friday and I'll get up about two hours earlier than usual, to accommodate her schedule as the mother of a toddler, and she'll come meet me at the coffee shop/bar that I can practically see from my apartment, to accommodate the fact that I will wake up about ten minutes before we are to meet. She lives across town, and always gets there first. I'll find her in our usual booth, under the stamped-tin ceiling and glowing orange bulbs that we all should be tired of by now but that give these mornings a sleepy, stolen, out-of-time feeling. We could have any kind of cocktail, if we wanted to, and although we never do, it's nice to know we could. It's nice to be surrounded by the colorful glass bottles and know that they can't hurt us. Instead we carefully tilt super-strong coffee into ourselves and talk about our writing, and about the absurdity and necessity of creativity under capitalism. And we gossip and we rant and we mourn, and we help each other figure out how to get to where we want to go. And we sometimes bring each other little presents, including these Chinese candies.

For a long time, we didn't know what the flavor was. Liz first gave them to me in a little satin drawstring bag, so I saw only their tiny wrappers, never the full package. She told me they were tangerine flavor, but there's a green citrus fruit right there on the wrapper of each one—a cut sphere holding neat geometrical segments, leaves unfolding from a curved stem, floating on a bright yellow background. When I pointed this out, she laughed and said, "I don't actually know, either, don't listen to me!" We agreed that we liked the mystery, even if it was a mystery that we could easily solve if we tried. It didn't really matter to me what the flavor was. They were my Liz candies.

Now, of course, here I am writing about them and I can't resist digging around. The flavor is chenpi, made from dried, fermented mandarin orange peel, traditionally used as both a cooking ingredient and a medicine to cure a range of symptoms, including digestive and respiratory ailments. It's one of the more common traditional medicines used in treating Covid-19 symptoms. This feels fitting to me, as those regular coffees with Liz were part of what helped me crawl out of the intense self-isolation into which I fell in the wake of the worst of the pandemic. There really is a candy for everything.

On Aero

I first encountered the Aero bar on the beaches of Australia, the year I studied abroad. It's a miracle, a blessing upon the earth. Its techno-strangeness renews your faith in the modern era.

I had thought, until today, that Aero was a Cadbury thing, and I could swear I've only recently seen it in the States. Turns out it dates to 1935, originally made by an old English company that Nestlé later took over. I'm confounded as to why these aren't standard in the checkout aisle.

Aero is a segmented chocolate bar with either more chocolate or a flavored filling inside (the best is mint), which has been aerated. This means that in cross section, the interior is full of tiny round holes, suggesting the texture of bone. It was even considered as a possible metaphor for a public health campaign, to help people understand the structures deep inside their own bodies.

I should hate this thing, with its illusion of plenty—the chocolate-filled one has the least possible chocolate per volume of any candy bar. (Respect to the reviewer who called it "a brutal hoax.") But what it lacks in volume it makes up for in the surface area of all those bubbles; its melt is incomparable, if fast. Hold a section in your mouth and feel it break down, chamber by chamber, your saliva flooding it like the compartments of the *Titanic*. It yields quickly, and each pocket is a tiny explosion of flavor. This bubbling feeling flies just below perception, tantalizingly elusive. Salman Rushdie himself called it "irresistibubble" when he worked an ad campaign for the bar in the 1970s, spawning the rumor that he had invented the candy. I love this alternate history: Rushdie making a bubbly candy bar while unknowingly enjoying his last few years of freedom from the fatwa.

On Caramel Apple Pops

A green apple lollipop, covered in the hard-chewy caramel that they pour over tart Granny Smiths and sell at the fair. A candy that imitates a fruit dressing up like a candy. *Ceci n'est pas une pomme au caramel.* Magritte would have loved it.

Purple

O h, the Whitman's Sampler. Another treat for
Christmas, or maybe for someone's birthday, and
yes, definitely for Valentine's Day, in its heart-
shaped incarnation.

The non-Valentine's Whitman's Sampler is a straw-yellow
box, colorfully decorated with faux cross-stitch—a scrolled
border with flowers in the corners, a little bird and a basket
of flowers floating in the center. "Whitman's" flies diagonally
across the middle, in embroidery font complete with carefully
drawn shadow. The word—its jaunty slant, the huge, ornate
W, the back-curving underline—broadcasts the exuberance
of men in old-timey ads: goateed Uncle Sam in his starry hat;
the Moxie pharmacist with his slicked pompadour; any big-
toothed, thumbs-up Mentos bro, all their hands gesturing
toward you, *This is what you need!* Whitman's! It is large! It
contains multitudes! The Sampler dates to 1912, a time when
people still remembered the reference for the name: a little
embroidery piece that showed off all the stitches that the

young lady could do. *Here's the delicious variety awaiting you. Come sit in the parlor and chat.*

The online food culture magazine *Eater* calls the Sampler "as normcore as candy gets, the chocolate equivalent of Jerry Seinfeld's dorky white high-tops," and they're not wrong. The Sampler was first distributed in pharmacies (just like Moxie) in cities and small towns across the country, and that's where Mom and I would buy it, at what was first a LaVerdiere's, an iconic Maine store that was later replaced by a Rite Aid. (I remember being bothered by the aggressive misspelling replacing the tantalizing French.) The Sampler was widely available; it meant that you didn't have to live in a town with a fancy confectioner's or a faux "dry goods" store to buy halfway decent chocolates.

Whitman's may seem basic today, but the company was a great innovator in its early years. The Sampler marked the first known use of cellophane to protect candy, and more than half a century earlier, in 1854, Whitman's had produced the first prepackaged candy: sugarplums in a decorative box. (Until then, candy was displayed on long counters or in jars or bins, and a clerk retrieved and packed each customer's selections.) These weren't sugared fruits, as you might have been picturing ever since childhood recitals of "While visions of sugarplums danced in their heads." The word "sugarplum" has long referred to a small, round hard candy, "plum" indicating its shape, and perhaps also the idea of something, according to Webster's, "excellent or superior of its kind."

While Whitman's first packaged candies might have been excellent or superior, the Sampler is really just decent—each serviceable, sugar-forward, and satisfying. There's a printed guide underneath the top cover, a search-and-find map telling

you which are caramel, which are cream-filled, which nougat. But it was more fun to wing it, even shut your eyes and pull one, Gump style. To see if the next one would be delicious enough to be the last one of the session, or if it would be some letdown (say, bland white nougat) propelling you to eat just one more, to end on a high note.

The Sampler item that was almost universally agreed to be disgusting was the jelly one. But I loved this thing, a gooey, purple gelatin covered in semi-dark chocolate, the fruit flavor kicking you in the salivary glands, the chocolate coating fragmenting when you bit it. It had a weird liqueur aroma and an unidentifiable berry tang—cherry or perhaps raspberry. (It's been discontinued.) I loved that everyone else hated it, that it was always there, one of the last standing, if I hadn't gotten to it yet. The standard Sampler had two of most flavors, so I had two candies set aside just for me, even in the box most meant for sharing. There would sometimes be a wasteful disappointment when someone accidentally took one and chomped into it, only to be disgusted. But usually I'd get the remaining half of that one, at least.

My choice of the jelly bonbon as favorite, when I would have told you even then that the caramels were objectively the most delicious, reveals my lifelong appreciation for the underappreciated. At our small, wood-paneled town library, I loved to take out books that no one had touched in years. I'd peek at the circulation card on the inside cover, and if the last stamp on, say, a canvas-backed book of poetry was from 1955, I'd take it home, no matter who wrote it. I resisted book recommendations, especially of contemporary novels, because, I reasoned, why did I need to read them if everyone else already was? They didn't need my attention. When we finally picked out a kitten and I was old enough to have a say, I insisted on the runt of the litter. And my current cat, Ziggy, is a wobbly cat, born with a small cerebellum, unable to toe a straight line or jump up on a bed. He lists and leans and occasionally flops over, like a drunk toddler. Adorable, but sort of the jelly bonbon of cats.

My second-favorite Whitman's, and the second most hated one, generally, was orange cream. Oh, the texture of this thing was wonderful—so grainy and sugary it exfoliated your tongue, orange the color of cheap sherbet. Sadly, I've since discovered, at a local candy shop, a high-class version of this candy that is one of the most delicious things I've ever tasted (thank you, Sweet Boutique in Tulsa, for importing Lake Champlain Chocolates from the East Coast), and now that more humble pleasure has been overwritten by something fancier and better, in a way I can't take back.

On Grape Starburst

These are an absence, a question—why don't they exist? There's an empty spot in the Starburst lineup, just waiting for them, part of the color spectrum missing. They would have the perfect chewy texture of Starburst, plus the assertive flavor of grape Bubble Yum, the pillow-soft gum that did not, in fact, contain spider eggs, as was rumored in the 1970s. It's a little sad that people thought there had to be some nefarious explanation for Bubble Yum's exceptional softness—the optimistic desire for magic conspiring with too-good-to-be-true pessimism to create yet another hysterical urban legend. As suspicious as people were of the innovative texture, I'm surprised so little attention was paid to the immersive flavor: the grape of grape Bubble Yum filled your nostrils from the second you peeled back the wrapper, and then, when you bit into it, flooded your entire sinus cavity, the flavor taking over every negative space in your head, as though you might taste manufactured grape for the rest of your life. You became the grape version of Violet Beauregarde, the girl who blows up blueberrily in Willy Wonka's factory, then gets fat-shamed in song.

There are plenty who have advocated for grape Starburst; it lives in the collective imagination along with the various fantastical candies Gene Wilder used to taunt his golden

ticket holders, each of them heartbreakingly unrealized. I'll never be able to sip a Fizzy Lifting Drink at a concert so I can see above tall men, or line my office in lickable wallpaper to keep me sustained while writing.

Then again, manifesting imagined pleasures does risk disappointment. Take, for example, Everlasting Gobstoppers, the candy most fated to be a letdown, forever unable to live up to its surreal origins. Our desires are doomed from the moment we enter Wonka's factory. It's run by a mad genius who employs only one race of people—the famed Oompa-Loompas—who seem not to have the benefit of a union, who live and sleep and work and die in an endless factory with no escape, maybe prevented from reproducing in some candy eugenics situation, but still sneaking a quick fuck occasionally in the boat tunnel, taking breaks only to disappear the remains of sacrificial children who break rules they didn't know existed, all for the purpose of making this one magical candy, a weird little ball of different shapes and colors that could be eaten forever without fading away, freeing the world's children from marshmallow tests and other restrictive tortures.

My memory took this concept of timelessness and ran with it, conflating the Gobstopper with Violet's three-course-dinner gum and pushing the concept even further, imagining a creation that summoned, in each moment, a distinct personal memory in the eater. Pop the Everlasting Gobstopper in your mouth and the first minute might taste like your mother's golden pancakes, the next like the salted caramel ice cream you licked on a first date. Moments later, you might taste the astringent grass and metallic hose water of a day on the Slip 'N Slide, or the fog that settled around your grandmother's house on the evening she died, bleak and sad but holding you as she once had. The additional powers I conferred on this already mystical, deathless candy now strike me as perfectly reasonable, for what is eternity without memory?

In truth, the Everlasting Gobstopper could do only one thing: last forever. But that was enough to make it a utopian ideal (though certainly not a Marxist one—let's not forget those Oompa-Loompas). Wonka sought to provide the world with a candy that would negate their need for any other; he tells his kiddo guests that he's made it "for children with very little pocket money." Poor kids would have a candy to accompany all their future memories, a way to sweeten any boring or difficult moment. And then, of course, Charlie is rewarded handsomely when he refuses to smuggle the Everlasting Gobstopper out to the evil capitalist Mr. Slugworth, even though the resultant cash could have saved his family from a poverty so dire they could afford only one bed for four grandparents.

The whole point of Wonka was that he'd found a point post-capitalism, post-sugar, past it, to eternal compassion and truth. To eat an Everlasting Gobstopper was to explode metaphysical limits in a synesthetic fugue state of emotional time travel. How could real-world, contemporary candy production begin to touch such an experience? Why would you set the bar there—why try to make this candy at all? Nestlé ignored Charlie's lesson about quick profit, deciding in 1976 to capitalize on the movie by bringing the Everlasting Gobstopper to the real world. What we got was this: little multicolored balls of sugar with tart centers, like gumball coating without the gum. They don't even last all that long.

What American kids like me didn't know was that only half the name was magical; gobstoppers have long been a category of candy in the UK—so long-lasting as to "stop your gob," i.e. silence your mouth. Here we call the same candy jawbreakers. Leave it to us to take something that conjures insult via word-play and turn it into a reference to physical violence.

If you really wanted the experience of a single piece of candy that would last a ridiculously long time, you could instead get one of those giant jawbreakers made of grainy rainbow layers. It was nearly the size of a baseball, far too large to do anything reasonable with (really, what is supposed to happen here? Are we to lick it like a deer?), and came in its own plastic case so you could haul it around while you worked on it over, what, weeks? The thing made a decent show of being everlasting, but eventually you didn't really care if it was. It felt like a homework assignment that would never end.

It's so tempting, the impulse to turn fantasy into reality, to turn imagination into experience. I recently discovered that people have been asking the grape Starburst question for years, and apparently they were answered in 2019 with Grape Slushie, part of the Summer Splash special edition of flavors. Sadly, it's been discontinued, fading into memory for the lucky few who ate it. I imagine them doomed, zombie-like, forever roaming the candy aisles, filled with fantastical, unquenchable desires.

On Vitafusion Melatonin Gummies, 5 mg

Almost Haribo-level smooth, with a slightly chewy spring, these are a menace. They bear a little golden seal proclaiming "Chef's Best Excellence 2019" (from the Chef's Best Excellence Awards?), and they are, good lord, too delicious. Royal purple and berry-flavored, these break my heart nightly, when I slip only one between my teeth, chewing as slowly as I can. I could eat enough of these to sleep for days, falling backward with my arms outstretched into a cloud of oblivion, hormones telling my body, again and again, "It's night, it's night, sleep on." An especially tempting fantasy as the world falls apart. After months of using these nightly—two weeks is meant to be the limit, according to the disingenuous label, directly opposite the golden award attesting to their deliciousness—my body no longer knows how to shut itself off. I'm candy dependent even when unconscious.

Rainbow Pastels

On Pastel Mints from the Bowl at
a Chinese Restaurant

A couple of times a year, my mother and I would drive down to Portland to go to the Planetarium, a bowl of darkness held under a stately dome on the University of Southern Maine campus. There in the bowl, the heat of humid summer lifted off us like invisible nebular dust as we settled in, tipping our vision up in the special tilt-back seats. For an hour or so, a deep velvety voice narrated the constellations for us, and when we walked back out into the light I would be stunned, there in the big city, feeling how expansive life was going to be as my body grew into the future, in the small slice of time afforded my human life.

After the Planetarium, we always headed to Polynesian Village, the sort of tiki-styled Chinese restaurant that was popular in the Northeast in those years. Cherrywood dragon carvings, zombie cocktails in Easter Island–head mugs, huge tropical fish tank, place mats with our Chinese zodiac signs, pupu platters with flaming "lava rock" at the center. It was

one of my favorite places in the world, dark and "exotic," and I liked myself for liking it. I can remember that feeling, an evaluation of my own potential for novelty and adventure. (Looking back as an adult, I would see the place as a white person's fantasy of a generalized Orient, a mishmash of cultural appropriation—China, for one thing, not being part of Polynesia; the dishes American-sugary—but it's also true that the Sings, who owned it, really were Chinese. And clearly knew what the locals wanted.) At the time, preferring the Polynesian over, say, Mario's Pizza showed that you were bound for the outside world, that you would leave Maine, maybe even see Hawaii someday.

I would eat a dozen or so fried chicken tenders, the breading wonderfully sweet and soft, and a few bright red teriyaki sticks, and cup after little cup of black tea. This was fine for a kid; it wasn't coffee, after all. Sometimes my mother's boyfriend, Dale, who I now wish had been my stepfather, if only for narrative efficiency, would have a zombie or two and get red-cheeked, laughing easily, and Mom had a drink she liked, too. Memory is hazy here, but it was probably a piña or strawberry colada. How strange, what one remembers on some days, what's completely obscured on others.

Dale never came to the Planetarium with us, and I now think that the whole trip might have been planned so he could conduct adult business that I wasn't supposed to know anything about, with men my mother wanted to keep me far away from. This doesn't diminish my joy at the memory of those Portland days. There's a satisfaction in learning the real meaning behind any childhood moment, even if that meaning is sad or scary. It takes these floating, isolated memories and pins them to the fabric of your life story, allowing you to better retain them within a greater context. Autobiography can be the greatest mnemonic. After the revelation comes vision: you can finally see the gap between your childhood understanding and your parents' perspective. A ragged seam you can stitch back together, even if they're gone.

Here's what Dale was: "my mother's boyfriend." The problem with this term is that it's about the relationship between the two of them, not between me and Dale. It's once removed. It also cannot convey that we all lived together for half a decade; "stepfather" would carry more temporal heft. And Dale did act like a __ father. He watched me while Mom was at work in the summer. He taught me to distinguish one fish from another, told me the name of each tree. I always felt safe when he drove. When we passed cows in the field, he would meow like a cat, to make me laugh. But if I wanted to go to a friend's house, I had to ask my mother, and she was likely the one who drove me there. She signed all the permission slips; she took me to the doctor. But the warmth of their relationship remains my best model for romantic love. If they'd gotten married, he would truly have been my stepfather—

a word that would belong to me, indicate belonging. A word that could still be true today.

At the end of the meal, stomachs stuffed, we'd each find a tiny bit more space for the fortune cookie, the three of us peering into a shared future where they grew old together and I swung out into the world, veering back occasionally like a comet. I'd do my best to ignore the dip in energy when the bill came, a small space of quiet that threatened to take hold, dropping us into the separate sadnesses of Sunday evening. But as we walked out, there it was: a cut-glass bowl of colorful mints. I loved those mints, and my excitement at this last little treat would put us all right again. When I was very small, I had to tilt my head up just to see them, unreachable and heavenly, until I grew tall enough to take the tinny little spoon and tip them out into my own hand. I'd take six or ten or so, or Dale would reach down and pour them into my eager paw— even, sometimes, after I could do it myself. You know the ones. They are pale pink and pale green and blue and white, crimped at the ends like pillows, and when you place one on your tongue it disintegrates almost immediately, melting into a flood of sugar, like syrup with a fine, satisfying grain to it, silty almost, the texture allowing your taste buds better purchase on the sweetness, the mint flavor a faint accent.

I would have another mint walking across the parking lot, and another as I got settled into the back seat of Mom's little car. She'd ask "All buckled?" and Dale would wait for my "Yep!" before he would even pull out of the parking spot. He would of course be the one driving, because they'd each had at least one drink and she was so very small, but we were in her car because it was safer than his old Firebird. So they worked together to hold me safely. I'd wait to eat the third mint until we were out on the road, crushing this one between my teeth, the back seat my private domain as yellow streetlights started rolling over my lap. Soon we left the city for the dark forested night, where I'd tip onto my back and glimpse stars out the rear window, the adults I loved happy up there in the front, Dale driving with one hand draped over the wheel at twelve o'clock, the other resting on Mom's pale, freckled thigh.

It's now twenty-five, thirty years later—long after their love ended, long after Mom died, long after Dale's arrests. Mom never saw the Polynesian close, in 1997, nor did she see the closing of the shoe factory where she worked, that same year. I do not know what her life would have looked like had it continued. The pandemic has made the idea of a communal bowl of naked candy inconceivable, and I've never eaten at Ghost Dragon Express, across the street from my apartment, so close I can see it from my desk. But I enjoy the smell when it wafts over, redolent of meat and scorched sugar. And I'm getting those mints the next time I see them, if I ever see them again. I miss the days when we could all dip into the same bowl, touching the traces of one another's hands, evidence that we all want more or less the same things, no matter what we call them.

On Candy Hearts

Pinching one of these between forefinger and thumb, I'm standing in a composite of all my elementary school classrooms. Sunshine filters through a wall of metal-trimmed windows along one side, heating vents gently breathing warm air at intervals along the hip-height counter below them. Between the vents, the counter holds marigold seedlings in tiny pots, a terrarium home to one friendly frog, a pile of slow-drying mittens. The light is multiplied by the low snowbanks outside, the flat field of white torn occasionally by the muddy marks of small feet. The sky is flat white or miraculous blue, a blue so electric we've almost forgotten it during all those darker days. Our teacher, brown curly hair permed and teased, stands at the blackboard demonstrating letters, her long arm moving gracefully over the curves, confidently striking through the *t*'s with perfectly straight lines. Or she's leaning back on her desk with a book in her hands, reading in a voice of utmost clarity, the voice of security itself. Or she's busy with her own work, head bent down, while we labor over spelling tests, doing our best to neatly fit the letters in where they belong. She looks up at us occasionally, to make sure we're all right.

On Valentine's, it feels like the whole day is devoted to love, but really it must be only a period or two. We're little, so we don't think about our day in instruction units, letting our teacher's plans carry us from one activity to another, with the exception of gym days, art days, music days. It's the 1980s

and all these days are still common in public school—there's still an understanding that education is about shaping people, humans, for wisdom and happiness, not just about training for future accomplishments leading to a well-paying job. So, too, is education still relaxed enough to include holiday celebrations. There are cookies brought from home, and no one's allergic to peanuts just yet. If I sound nostalgic, I am. But of course, the holiday calendar was uncritically Christian, exclusionary. Nostalgia is rarely innocent.

On Valentine's, though, the day was sweet. Your mom bought you a box of little paper cards at the pharmacy sometime the week before, and maybe she helped you fill them out. She asked you who your friends were and reminded you to include the teacher, if you didn't on your own. Maybe she asked if there was a boy you liked, even if she herself didn't like only boys. Or she left you to your own devices in your room for a while, so you could fill out *To: Robbie. From: It's a Secret. To: Stephanie. From: Your friend, Sarah.* You'd parse each card for romance, categorizing them—on this one, two cartoon puppies really kissed, creating a little heart explosion. That one meant something; you couldn't send it to just anybody. This one, the kitten with big, friendly eyes who says "Let's be friends!"—safe for sending to all.

You'd come in that morning and deposit your valentines in a big shoebox decorated in pink wrapping paper, and at some point, probably during recess, your teacher would distribute them. Later, during the party, when the candy came out, you'd get to check your mailbox or cubby and finally see who'd thought of you. Girls compared, whispering with their heads together: who got the most, who got one from a boy. I wonder what boys thought, not so raised in anticipation of romantic love. Some would have considered the day tedious, silly. Others would secretly hope for a message, and have no one to eagerly share that hope with. Each year, I longed for a secret admirer, even more than I wished for a missive from any single boy. A secret admirer could be anyone, and in the space between mystery and discovery lay all the possibilities for perfect romance. A secret admirer couldn't let you down by hocking a loogie while waiting for the bus at the end of the day, or by saying that girls couldn't run as fast as boys, or by disliking cats.

Along with valentine cards, candy hearts served as currency. A little box of them was a freighted thing: if you poured them into someone's hand and KISS ME came tumbling out, you might blush, revealing your fantasy that someone, someday, would kiss you, maybe even this person. From the age of seven or eight onward, I'd listen to the tortured love songs of the eighties, riding along with my mother in our little car with the windows rolled down, and suffer vicariously, gloriously, wishing I could be addicted to love or proving that love is a battlefield or swooning under the spell of the magic man. The day when I would finally be kissed would be the BEST DAY, and then we'd be together FOR EVER. There in the classroom, or alone reading in my room, I'd pick out a candy heart, maybe BE MINE or NEW LOVE, and flip it over onto my tongue, melting down and absorbing the message, like a spell for future love. A secret spell, contained only within myself.

On Necco Wafers

I just cannot believe that anybody truly likes these. Like refined Tums. The colors are beautiful, though, and they hold

up well to heat. The wax paper has a nice crafty feel. Okay for travel, in a pinch. Overall, annoyingly harmless.

Of course, much of what feels innocent today was challenging in its day. Necco wafers are arguably the oldest commercially produced American candy, hitting the scene in 1847. This is the early Victorian era, people. The Model T wouldn't roll out for another half century. Candy was one of the first industrialized foods, produced far from one's kitchen, from one's town, under a cloak of corporate secrecy. It represented modern convenience but also sparked anxiety—what exactly were we eating?

In the mid-nineteenth century, production methods were becoming more sophisticated, creating candy in bright colors, strange textures, and intense flavors that had never been possible in wholesome homemakers' kitchens. The huge popularity of penny candy, a pleasure children could obtain independently, made parents nervous, and temperance organizers claimed that sugar was priming kids to drink. (We've recently learned that candy doesn't even make kids hyperactive. Sorry, they're just buzzed at the birthday party because they're having fun.) Some even went so far as to claim that eating candy and drinking were essentially the same thing, since both sugar and alcohol are carbohydrates, differing only in the arrangement of their molecules. Candymakers would seize on this "research" to offer their creations as alternatives to alcohol during Prohibition, a marketing angle that I imagine makes a lot of sense to several of my sober friends whose AA journey included an ice cream phase. Candy has been denigrated during all three clean-living movements in the United States, periods when people became preoccupied with health and wellness, and when "natural" living was considered especially moral and virtuous. If this sounds familiar to you, it's because you're in one. If it sounds repressive, I agree.

On Pixy Stix

These always seemed vaguely forbidden, inappropriate. First, the two *x*'s, connoting porn, or at least hair metal bands—leather pants, sweat, smeared eyeliner on hard-femme men. It's no wonder older kids tried to snort them, or there was an urban legend that you could—did anyone ever actually do this?

Pixy Stix were a pure, fine powder, rolled up in a paper cylinder, and as such separated kids into two camps: those who knew that they resembled drugs and those innocents who had no idea.

I was in the first camp. I'd seen Dale at the kitchen counter, pulling open capsules and carefully spilling their powders on a sheet of green-edged glass. That's as far as I got before my mother whisked me away, although I must have seen people doing lines of coke in movies when I was very, very young, before anyone understood that toddlers might store memory, even of things they didn't yet understand. I was well acquainted with our basement garden, a custom-built closet where Dale grew only one kind of dark green, spiky-leaved plant, under clear white lights made brighter by silver fixtures that looked like Mom's aluminum mixing bowls. I'd sit down there with him sometimes while he tended his plants, and we'd decorate them together with tiny frogs and gnomes on sticks. He'd let me direct the project, placing one in the dark, cool soil, one high up in the crook of a branch. I never thought to ask why these plants weren't out in the sunshine with the others, in the large garden Dale had built on the side of the house, with the tomatoes and the cukes and the marigolds.

I had some sense, though, that I shouldn't mention the basement garden to my friends, and it was this sense, just under awareness, that hinted at something untoward about Pixy Stix. Always more of a chocolate kid, I never sought these out, but they would come to me, in party favor bags or handed over by a generous classmate. And of course I would eat them, because they were sugar, after all. I'd rip off one end of the paper and tip the stick over and pour, right onto the membrane under my tongue, feeling something desperate about it, or rather the weirdly fun imitation of desperation. It was best to dump out as much as you could at one time, because with each serving you got the open end a little wetter, until the wrapper dissolved into a nasty little ball of paper and sugar that you had to rip off to get at the rest. When the powder hit, my salivary glands would jump, rushing and flooding, and then I'd swallow the sugar paste, in strawberry or lime or grape, the flavors blunt, more red/green/purple than anything resembling a fruit.

Pixy Stix now come in clean plastic cylinders, and you can inhale weed legally through a smokeless USB drive that looks like a Bond gadget. I miss old hot rods rumbling in the driveway, the itchy stalks of tomato plants, seeing around the edges of things because adults think you're too young for memory.

On Candy Necklaces

These don't taste good. Nobody ever claimed they did, but nobody ever addresses the fact that although these are technically candy, technically edible (nontoxic, at least, we can assume), there's no real pleasure in eating them. They are sugar and chalk and color, a little flavor, if you strain. But as they are sugar, so they are candy, and the idea of the candy necklace is that it's always there—you can have candy anytime you want. Candy in class, candy on the swing set, candy in the back seat of your mom's car. Candy in the outfield, candy in the stacks. All you had to do was pull the stretchy length of sugar beads off your neck and up into your mouth, bite one off, and chew.

There's something a little sexy about candy necklaces, or

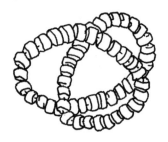

something pre-sexy. That you could just bite food off your own body—or someone else's—at any moment kept all forms of appetite ever present. Is it natural to think of body-as-consumable as sexy, or is this capitalism informing my desire, all of our desires? A candy necklace is commerce and candy and nascent desire coming together in the preteen body. The end point of this is the candy G-string, just a big triangle of the necklace candies. There is no way to make this look sexy: it's just an unflattering lump, and there's no way, unless you are extremely flexible, to eat them off yourself, to perform an alluring self-cannibalism. We must think of this as a product for straights, in its Joey-from-*Friends* basic combinatory logic—*Pussy? Good! Candy? Good!*—and so, props for encouraging men to go down, I guess. But you have to bite these. Get those teeth away from me.

On Wax Bottles

Little kids will always prefer three nickels over two dimes, and this same appreciation of quantity over value contributes to the love of wax bottle candies. Eating them is like drinking one teeny tiny soda after another: bite the wax top off, then suck

out the brightly colored candy gel. These are called Nik-L-Nips and originally cost, you guessed it, a nickel. Since the filling is such a tiny shot of sugar, these feel overpriced to me, even as cheap as they are. They would have been an even worse value for kids of the early twentieth century, when a nickel, that most awkward of coins, was apparently worth something.

You're supposed to chew the wax like gum after sucking out the gel, but when I was growing up, nobody was ever sure if the wax was actually safe, so we just chucked out the used husks. They didn't taste like much, and the whole experience was more fun than delicious, imagination working overtime to create the flavor. The feeling of becoming giant, the soda bottles becoming chewy—an Alice-in-Wonderlandian adventure.

On Smarties

Before we begin, let's acknowledge that we're in confusing territory.

First, we have to set aside SweeTarts, which come in various forms—half-inch, chewy disks in a movie box, as well as slightly chalky, pinkie-end-size disks stacked in a row of ten or so and wrapped in clear plastic. It's the latter form that resembles Smarties, here in the United States, but in the UK and Australia there is an entirely different candy called Smarties. It's a chocolate-and-candy-shell thing, the inspiration for M&M's, produced in 1941 and immediately sent off with World War II soldiers.

Now that the comparison has been raised, I need to take a side and assert that Smarties are better than SweeTarts, if only to align myself with what is still a family company. SweeTarts date to 1962 and, like most candy brands, have since been gobbled up by an international corporation. Smarties date to 1949, and the company is run by the three granddaughters of its founder. They are still in New Jersey, that bastion of midcentury candy production, and the formula has changed little. Old-fashioned candies like these call to mind piers stretching out over slate-blue East Coast water, dates in cars dragging a small-town midwestern strip, soda fountains and gas stations surrounded by mesquite desert, the whole problematic colonial, white, Americana imagery, and I recognize the championing of small business as capitalist indoctrination at its core, the Smarties story even about an immigrant who made good, but still, I prefer the Dee sisters, laughing in the sunshine in the *New York Times* with their smiling, big-eared grandpa, over Ferrero SpA, the second-largest candy conglomerate in the world.

Smarties are categorized as a wafer candy, but they are harder than Necco wafers or candy hearts, with more integrity. If you get some traction on them with a bite or a tooth grind, they will melt a little, and they are wonderfully just the size of a molar. They come in a clear plastic sleeve of twenty or so candies, the plastic twisted at the ends, and the packaging is cheekily meta: printed on the sleeve, just smaller than the product itself, is a picture of a sleeve of Smarties, end twists and all, and it's this picture that carries the "Smarties" name, a sweet, unnecessary mise en abyme. The Smarties in the picture of Smarties are brightly colored, unlike the candies themselves, which are pleasing shades of pastel.

Each Smartie is a disk with a smooth, concave bowl on each side for the tip of your tongue or your finger, a shape that anticipates the body. The flavor is fine—gentle and sweet (not tart at all)—sugar plus a faraway hint of unidentifiable fruit, a princess-and-the-pea vibration of cherry or grape or orange. Apparently the yellow one is pineapple; who knew?

These are perfect for throwing into a Halloween bag or bucket, or for scattering among grab bags at the birthday party of your most spoiled classmate. When I would twist one open as a kid, I'd try to keep the row together, setting it on its side like a row of tires, picking each one up with thumb and forefinger. Their hardness allows for an indefinite extension of the five-second rule. They are not a good pocket candy;

it's too easy for the roll to come unrolled, Smarties escaping into your pants pocket, inevitably getting crushed and leaving sticky candy dust in there for your mom to deal with. Same for backpacks: travelers beware. But they keep forever and can linger in harder, more protected locations, like a car's glove box, for when low blood sugar and the New Jersey traffic threaten to make you snap at your partner in the passenger seat right at the start of a rare weekend trip, when you really need something to keep things sweet.

On SweeTarts

I just noticed the "sweetheart" in these if you say it aloud, extra sweetness hiding in the word. On the box, "TARTS" is capitalized to make the portmanteau legible, although the *T* rather disappears at the bridge between two words, hovering over a dividing line of two colors, and so "ARTS" also appears prominently. The art of blending the sweet and the tart, easy pleasure with a bite.

Here's the basic SweeTarts lineup, excluding holiday specials and other innovations: the Smarties copycat roll, the movie box with chewy disks, and the big, extra-chewy wafers that come four to a pack. The best known and best tasting is the movie box kind, whose structure and size resembles a Mento squished down into a flat disk. There's a harder, more sugary outside, glossy, with deep colors, and a chewy inside, where the tartness lives. Once you get there, your mouth is coated in sugar, so the flavors are pretty evenly balanced, just like the logo promises.

There was a period of a few months in late childhood when I opted for these instead of Junior Mints or Milk Duds at the movies. Probably Mom offered me one of those and I said, "No, I want SweeTarts," not to be contrary but to throw her off, to be unknown. Preteens, in pulling away from their parents to become their own people, must become unknown, in whatever small ways they can. I was so close to my mother, and our relationship so sweet, who knows what horrible things I would have done to get further from it, if given the time. If she had said, "SweeTarts, really?" I would have rolled my eyes, no doubt, and become annoyed. She might have felt dismayed at my changing, in anticipation of all the larger ways I would change. Although I wish she were still here, sometimes I'm glad we didn't have to go through all that, that we never had to, piece by piece, let each other go.

Rainbow Brights

On Skittles

S kittles implore you to "taste the rainbow"—a phrase so wonderfully gay and sexy I'm surprised that, when I go looking, I find no good Skittles memes, even in June.

Skittles are like a pellet version of Starburst, little ovular pastilles like Go pieces, in colors from flat school-bus yellow to Ursula purple. They've managed to innovate without embarrassing themselves, particularly in the Tropical pack, the flavors bright and delicious, the non-primary colors an extra enticement.

A bag of Skittles opens too easily, and a few will always escape. It is this sort of candy flotsam that, I would later find out, charmed Preston in our early days. We moved in together after only three or so months of dating. We had a deep, instinctive understanding of each other, a sort of matched vibration and a robust reading list overlap, but now, eight years later, I understand we barely knew each other. Everyone knows this—that moving in early is a huge gamble, bigger than you can possibly appreciate at the time, that you don't yet know

this person's daily habits, the tiny things that might so grate on you as to be unendurable, the snoring and the musty towels and the inability to take the trash out eventually gaining enough snowball momentum to end a great love. This list is clichéd, with more than a hint of gender, and even while those exact annoyances are piling up, you know this, and you feel like you should be smarter than to care, and this sort of friction feels all the more undignified and pathetic for its predictability, for showing you the hubris of your honeymoon period, but when it comes down to it, life is the little details. How we spend our days is how we spend our lives, as Annie Dillard told us years ago, and who wants to spend their life doing more than their share of the laundry? This is all putting aside whether or not you'll discover your love to be subtly manipulative or definitely narcissistic or just too immature to be a good partner.

Miraculously, we have found none of these major flaws in each other, although I'm sure we've both had moments of doubt—have I mentioned he doesn't eat candy? Like at all? So far, we've found the daily stuff to be more charming than vexing, in the balance. You learn a lot about yourself in the process of living with a person, and what I've learned is that not all adults eat candy all the time. In the early months,

Preston would turn out my pockets while doing laundry, or reach his hand into the side of the car door, and find those little Skittles package corners, or the cellophane twists of Goetze's Bulls-Eyes, or he'd open the trash can lid to dump out the previous day's coffee grounds and find a veritable snowfall of Werther's wrappers. He never found the candy itself, because it rarely stayed long enough in the house. He found all this very charming, and said so. "The variety!" he exclaimed. He started asking me what I thought of each, and I'd review them and go off on tangents and, well, here we are. Sometimes you have to take it on faith that if you please at least one person, others will want to listen, too. I am continually grateful to live with this first reader, one who helps me see when I'm having an idea, who is always curious about me, who takes pleasure in my pleasure without needing a bite for himself. And he's cute.

On Runts

Runts were the candy runt version of fruits—tiny, hard, technicolor bananas, cherries, strawberries, oranges, and limes. Perfect little gems of flavor, with none of that messy peeling, no risk of getting an unripe strawberry, no revolting orange pith to scrape off with your fingernails. Their clean aesthetic appealed as the internet would soon appeal—its hard lines and bright screens, the dramatic glamour of the kids in *Hackers,* the future frictionless and neat. The illusion of their antiseptic surfaces was carried through to their delivery mechanism, most often a vending machine at the blessed end of the grocery checkout line, or in the waiting room at the mechanic's, or at

the laundromat, where you waited with your mom through biweekly afternoons and longer, through months or years of saving for a washer or—dream bigger—a house that had one. You'd put a quarter into the slot and turn the crank hard and the miniature fruits would cascade down the chute, pushing against the metal flap with their weight. You had to be quick, cup your other hand under the exit, then carefully lift that little door and let them spill into your hand, a bounty like the shining rain of quarters falling into the palms of slot machine victors on TV. Then you just ate them, bare from the machine, from your overflowing hand.

Runts and the quarter-crank machines that spewed them out were a blessing upon an only child, and I hope they don't become one more sad, small loss of this time, slipping unseen beneath the waves of bigger catastrophes. I hate to consider the machines' disappearance, to think that kids no longer would get to experience that brilliant surprise: candy on an unexpected horizon, easily accessible in those non-places and idle times between one parental chore and another. All you had to do was get Mom to pause for a second, give you one shiny quarter in a moment when she was harried and vulnerable, perhaps feeling guilty for dragging you along, separating you from both homework and play, guilty, too, for not staying married, for not having another kid to keep you company, guilty for getting pregnant so young, for dropping out of school, guilty for her own occasional pleasures, her sugary impulses. It was almost too easy, the low-hanging runt fruit of candy hunting, purchased with a few leftover cents, an illusion of excess. Then you could sit, pleased with your catch and with your powers of persuasion, riding along in the passenger seat listening to Led Zeppelin on the radio, watching Mom relax now that you both were out of that long line, money budgeted and spent, the stress of balancing the numbers on her little calculator now passed, the deed done.

Each runt was a solidly concentrated flavor, immersive— the banana so banana, the lime so lime—and if you ate them one by one you could mark out all kinds of time, you could occupy an hour, maybe, sitting there while your mother's boyfriend quietly fumed because they'd just started the oil change, right when they'd said it would be ready, the shop not too far from the house but too far, really, to go home and come back later. To occupy the time, he had only old issues of *Popular Mechanics* or, in Maine, the *Uncle Henry's,* a black-and-white newsprint circular full of classified ads, mostly old-ish cars and trucks for sale, each a fantasy of an upgrade from the one you'd brought in. But you were a kid, and you had a bright pile of candy, and anyway you liked the smell of motor oil and brake dust, rubber like a warm low note in the summer, although you won't think about why until years later, when hazy preschool memories of visiting your father's garage return to you. You'll just sit quietly and enjoy each shot of sugar—the orange so orange, strawberry a tiny bright heart of berry.

On Those Colorful Little Buttons on Paper

Apparently these have a name, or names, not that anyone has ever cared. They are, in fact, Candy Buttons. They're also called candy dots or, grossly, pox. The internet tells me they were first introduced in Williamsburg, Brooklyn, by a J. Sudak and Son at the beginning of the twentieth century. I love that. Stickball, running in sprinklers, the old Brooklyn people can't stop telling us was so different, the one that sits forever projected upon your own streetscape, part of the romance that won't let you leave. Back when warehouses warehoused, and children were appeased by a pure sugar dot (or "rounded peg") welded onto a strip of paper.

These came in three flavors—cherry, lemon, and lime—but I only ever tasted sugar and chalk. It was impossible to peel them off cleanly; you had to first melt the paper off with your tongue and then either swallow the soggy scrap or pull it off and flick it to the ground. Necco eventually bought them out. Of course.

I'm filing these firmly under Halloween Disappointment Candy. I'd smile back at the gray-haired donor of these

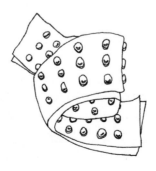

paper strips because my mother was standing next to me, while thinking, *Honestly, who's too cheap to buy a Hershey's variety pack?* These things could have been sitting around since the stickball days and you'd never know.

I would always eat them, though—not for the flavor but for the color. The pinks were perfectly, glowingly hot pink, the yellows not sallow but hopeful, the blues both bright and clear, like little nubs of pool-swimming joy.

On Sour Patch Kids Heads

I'm not a big fan of sour things, and historically have liked Sour Patch Kids only after the sour dust is melted off, when they become a rather excellent sweet gummy. Time makes them sweeter. They're a thing I've eaten because they're there, because someone has offered them to me, and they are, after all, still candy.

Recently, however, I encountered an exceptional variety of Sour Patch Kids called Heads. Once again, I had Sophie to thank for introducing me to a new gummy. Preston and I and Sophie and her younger sister Mo, who for a time was my roommate in New York, were sitting up late, drinking wine in the sisters' apartment on Cape Cod, when Sophie pulled out a bag of these Heads. Her best friend, Ori, had given her one, propelling Sophie to search for more at the shop where Ori had bought them. Sophie, who runs a restaurant and is thus disinclined to be rude to anyone in a service position, had stared at a big wall of candy, not finding them, and then demanded of the owner, behind the counter: "Is this all you

have?" He shrugged. She got Ori on video call, held up her phone, and said, "See this girl? She was just in here yesterday; she bought these Heads. Don't you have them?" He did not, nor could she impress upon him his responsibility, as a purveyor of candy, to either provide or explain. By the time I visited, Sophie had bought a dozen packs online. She has excellent taste. But I already knew that.

It sometimes happens that people offer me candy I don't particularly want, and I feel compelled to take and eat it, if only to maintain my sugar-hound identity. This makes me worry that I'm not terribly interesting, that I have made a preference into a personality, but no matter. I took a Head, for reputation maintenance and because rejection of any proffered food is one of the more alienating human interactions. I was also curious about this candy that had led kind and considerate, vegetarian healthy eater Sophie to confront a shopkeeper. The first gummy was excellent: much less sour than your standard Sour Patch Kid, the flavor more an accent than a mouth-strafing burn. These are whole Kids, but larger and flatter. The Head for which they're named balloons above the body and is a different color and flavor than the rest of the Kid: three varieties with two flavors each. The best is peach-cherry, which is green and red. When it melted down smooth, it tasted exactly like the better Swedish Fish.

On Blow Pops

What's happier than a Blow Pop? They come in bright fruit flavors—grape, strawberry, Blue Razz Berry (whatever that is), cherry, watermelon, sour apple . . . The list goes on and on, becoming ever more abstract: What-a-Melon, Black Ice. Sixteen flavors at the time of this writing! What generosity, what wild, excessive variety. Black Ice: What are we even talking about here? Crazzberry. Candy Corn.

Inside we have a hunk of gum in only one flavor: bubble gum. Look how we've taken the action and form of a thing and made it the name of a flavor. Gum of other flavors can bubble, too, but we all know what we mean here: a vaguely strawberryish situation, tempered with unidentifiable herbal extracts.

The story of how bubble gum flavor came to be—and the whole history of commercially produced American chewing gum—is wild, before you even consider the manufacturing innovations that allowed people to put it on a stick and surround it with hard candy. Chewing gum as we know it today was inspired by General Antonio López de Santa Anna—yes, Santa Anna of the Alamo, the Mexican president who went on to become an autocrat known for such wacky stunts as holding a state funeral for his amputated leg, a bizarro incident I just barely remember from the entire year of Texas history I was compelled to suffer through while living with my mean aunt Tootsie in junior high, after I was sent out west in the wake of my mother's death. By the 1850s (after Texas became an independent republic, a fact certain Texans will not let you forget) Mexico had tired of Santa Anna's antics (Santa Antics?), and he found himself exiled to, of all places, Staten Island. He brought with him his stock of chicle, the resin of the sapodilla tree, chewed for centuries by the Maya and the Aztecs and, eventually, other groups in Mexico. ("Chicle" still remains the Spanish word for chewing gum.)

Santa Anna tasked local inventor Thomas Adams with developing chicle into a substitute for rubber, then a hugely lucrative commodity, in a ploy to rebuild his fortune and regain power in Mexico (optimistic, considering he was seventy-four already, but as we're currently learning in the United States, autocrats who build their personas on publicity stunts will never stop seeking power, particularly after they've lost it, no matter their age). Adams could not get chicle to vulcanize—become hard enough for use in tires, etc.—and

Santa Anna eventually returned, powerless, to Mexico City, dying soon afterward.

But the chicle story didn't end with Santa Anna. Adams, left with a supply of the stuff and $30,000 into the project, eventually got the idea to turn it into chewing gum by boiling it down to purify it and, most importantly, adding flavors. He chose black licorice—the flavor would come to be called Black Jack—and Tutti-Frutti, a combination of fruits under the moniker that then referred to a popular ice cream flavor. These were smart choices: a bold, astringent flavor and something mellow and pleasant, appealing and vague, which would become the basis for our conception of gum flavor going forward. ("Bubble gum" flavor now means various combinations of artificial, industrial flavorings, which in turn can be mimicked at home by mixing natural strawberry, banana, pineapple, cinnamon, wintergreen, clove, and other extracts—the organic becoming synthetic becoming organic again.) The resulting product was superior to gums then on the market, which, made from paraffin or spruce sap and plagued with impurities, did not much resemble what we enjoy today. In 1888 Adams placed America's first vending machines on subway platforms to give commuters something to do while they read the paper and ignored their fellow New Yorkers. A decade later, he partnered with William Wrigley Jr. and others to form the American Chicle Company, which would make Chiclets and Dentyne.

Like countless other things people in the United States consider quintessentially "American," chewing gum's original cultural roots have been obscured by industrialization and commodification. The world has Indigenous peoples to thank for a product so ubiquitous in daily life and popular media that we barely notice it (see also: the Mesoamerican roots of chocolate; see also: chicle used as early dental fillings). Sapodilla trees would eventually be overfarmed and synthetic replacements would step in, although some gums are still made with chicle, notably Glee, which I confess I don't much like, as it loses its flavor in approximately twenty-eight seconds.

Thomas Adams made gum gummy—stretchy and malleable and soft—but he did not make it bubble. Dubble Bubble is the original bubble gum, developed in 1928 and based on a 1906 gum called Blibber-Blubber. It was colored pink because that was the only color additive present in the factory when it was created. Dubble Bubble is now the hardest gum in existence, but hey, credit where it's due, because that pink sure had staying power, and bubbling is brilliant.

The gum in Blow Pops is, unfortunately, thin, with poor structure, and awful for blowing bubbles, although I was never super good at that anyway. File with jumping rope and hula-hooping under femme skills I could never nail as a kid. But Blow Pops were originally enjoyed in a masculine context, included in US combat rations in World War II, when 25 percent of candy production went to soldiers overseas as easy, quick energy in the field. Sweetness and bubbles in the midst of terror and trauma. Sweetness as survival. When the troops came home, they still craved what had brought them tiny shots of happiness amid the chaos, and Blow Pops and M&M's and other wartime candies boomed in popularity. It is breathtaking to think of how many of our apparently simple pleasures are connected to violence.

On Gumdrops

I ate gumdrops mostly in very early childhood, on fall afternoons when my babysitter, a woman a little older than my
mother, named Peggy, would take me to her much older
friend's house to visit. The friend had puffy white hair and
lived in a little house or apartment near the elementary
school, on a sort of backstreet, across the way from what
I thought of then as the Army Building. It was a one-story
red-brick building behind a basic chain-link fence.

What I mean to say is that the building wasn't forbidding,
and now I'm wondering what it even could have been—a re-
cruitment office? A National Guard facility (but for what)?
It was just there, the sort of landmark you know you'll never
interact with, and, most importantly, it had a big, inviting red
maple out front that would drop its slick maroon leaves on
the cement sidewalk where I would ride my bike with Mom.
It sticks in my mind, this building, because now it strikes
me as strange that an apparatus of war, however indirect,
sat right there on a leafy street in my town. But when Peggy
brought me, we'd pull up across the street in her little car,

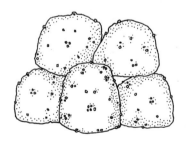

and now that I've thought through all these other details, I remember—it just came back to me this second—that the old woman's name was Dot. She had a big, black mole on her face, and even as a very young kid I appreciated the easy logic, Dot marked with a dot. It is these sorts of coincidences that allow very young children to dream that there is order in the universe.

Dot had an airless, too warm house—deep beige carpet, softly ticking clocks—and she always had gumdrops in a heavy cut-glass bowl. (They were the sugar-coated kind and thus not, as would be better for the story, the brand called Dots.) Going there felt like being wrapped in a blanket, nothing much to do but sit on the hard couch while the adults talked and carefully pluck little handfuls of sugar nuggets from the bowl. I liked biting them in half and observing the tiny furrows my teeth made in the gelatin, the cherry or lemon shining clear against the diffuse light from the sugar coating. I must have brushed that loose sugar off my hands, onto that couch or carpet, but no one ever bothered me about it. I was a cute blond kid, a little sensitive, the sort who could barely stand to wear socks because of the sensation of the front seam on my toes, but otherwise agreeable, and Dot, I think, liked having a young person in her house. This must have been why Peggy visited her with me in tow.

These visits to Dot's candy bowl seem dreamlike, too early for memory, but it turns out that my memory stretches back even further than I'd thought. All my life I've recalled how one time at the grocery store with Peggy—perhaps on our way home from Dot's—I was monkeying around on the metal railing between the checkout aisles (which I suppose were meant to corral shopping carts) and I flipped upside down and cracked my head. All these years later, having seen my medical records from the hospital, I've learned that I was only three years old. For much of my early adulthood, I had sort of proudly proclaimed that I could remember nothing before the age of seven or eight. To me, this seemed interestingly unusual, or laudably adult, or pleasingly art monster, as though I were a person who didn't need the years before she could write. But I remembered the day in the grocery store, if not the hospital visit afterward, and I still remember, too, Dot with the gumdrops, and I wonder if there are other early childhood memories I might have mistaken for dreams.

On Old-Fashioned Grandmother Candy

I'm at a loss for what else to call this, but everyone thirty-five and up has eaten it. This is a variety of hard (but not super hard) candy that comes in a big tin, sometimes at the holidays but not always. It's maybe Italian. There are candy spheres and candies shaped like little fruits (mostly raspberries) and one-inch sticks like candy canes with cut-off ends. The last of these are striped in various colors, some with a weird surprise chocolate filling. They call to mind a *Mister Rogers* episode where he visits a candy factory and watches as ribbons of molten, stretchy sugar get pulled and worked into candy canes. Remember that one? I do, but it turns out that it doesn't exist. (Maybe we're thinking of the candy-colorful crayon factory visit?) There's no trace of candy in the official list of episodes, and there's even an article circulating on the internet about a boy who wrote to Mister Rogers to suggest he visit the Ghirardelli factory, only to be turned down. In his

reply letter Fred wrote, "Even though candy can be a fun snack once in a while, we wouldn't want to give so much attention to candy on our television visits." Not even Mister Rogers was perfect.

This message—that candy was only for every once in a while—was mostly absent from my mother's house. Sugar was surely the least of her worries, and her sweet tooth was nothing compared with mine, so she had never really had to think about restricting it for herself. She enjoyed the occasional Peppermint Pattie, sure, but her brain didn't light up when chocolate melted on her tongue. Candy didn't give her the happiness that it gave me, the soothing feeling that everything was okay, but she could see it in me, and she could not deny me. She was incredibly thin, and muscled from her factory work, a sort of red-haired Sarah Connor hidden in a tiny town. I started worrying about my weight at age seven, angry at my chubby thighs. I had some sense that I should limit what I ate, but no idea how to do such a thing. Instead I took blue Bic pens and defaced the models on the covers of Mom's *Redbook* and *Marie Claire* magazines, blacking out teeth and adding devil horns, full of a bitterness I did not yet understand.

Grammy was like me, with her ever-present tin of colorful

candies, boxes of sugar-sparkling grocery store doughnuts on the counter, jugs of grape soda in the fridge. When I wasn't feeling well, she'd give me ginger ale—ultra-sweet Schweppes, which did make me feel better, at least emotionally. She didn't bake and she didn't knit, although she did garden, growing zinnias next to her door and tomato plants down the gentle slope of her backyard. Her most grandmotherly feature was her body: small shoulders, a slight stoop, and a round belly that I loved hugging while pressing my face into her slick polyester tops. Grandmothers were *supposed* to be soft, I thought. But she made it clear that her softness was a problem—she felt fat. I wouldn't learn until later that she'd struggled with her weight all her life, and of course she had—she had twelve children and that sweet tooth, and she was most certainly not one to exercise. (She didn't like sweating because it messed up her hair.)

The revelation wasn't that Grammy had been round in her youth. The important insight was that she remained preoccupied with her weight because she had never gotten to be thin as a young woman. Her clock had run out. And so she passed the pressure on down to us, my mother and me, both still young enough to enjoy being thin and beautiful. If Mom could stay that way. If I could ever get that way. They both loved me via food, and even as I dipped into those rattling tins of colorful candy, I'd hear my mother feebly defending me against Grammy's observation that I was "getting pretty chunky" (a charge that for me ruined the raisin-and-peanut bar that went by the same name).

I'm putting a lot of pressure on my grandmother, a woman who suffered decades of abuse, who never got to pursue higher education, who never learned to drive a car. And the truth is, I didn't live with my grandmother full time. What of the weakness of Mom's replies? What about the doctor's note I have right here next to me, from when she was hospitalized with pneumonia, calling her "anorexic"? I feel angry reading this. *This guy doesn't know what he's talking about,* I think. But then I keep thinking about it. None of my aunts are thin quite like she was. I vividly remember her buying an exercise bike and then ceasing its use because it made her legs "even bigger." And just the other day, I figured out why I like the taste of apples but also find them really annoying: as I got older, they became Mom's go-to healthier offering when I wanted a sweet snack. She knew how much not being thin tortured me. She was just trying to help. And now I look back and think: *Did* she have body image issues? Or is my memory of her body a repository for my own?

I did reach my mother's thinness—twice, actually. The first time was in my immediate grief, when the pressures of junior high plus the strict demands I placed on myself pushed me down to a size zero. The second time was twenty years later, when I published my book about Mom and my doctor put me on the antidepressant Wellbutrin—widely known as the "happy, horny, skinny pill." (I was two of those things, because instead of "happy" I'd say "energetic.") The drug plus the book release made me so anxious I barely ate, and I worked out endlessly and my weight plummeted, and I still think about it— how I knew I was too thin, how it made my face look older, how I loved how my jeans hung while feeling shame about the fatphobia that compelled that love, how publishing that book felt so huge, so overwhelmingly in-the-world, that I wanted to be agile and light, something that could slip between the cracks, a completely different animal from the chubby little kid who'd eaten whole tins of candy in her grandmother's kitchen, a place that no longer existed.

I loved feeling small but densely powerful in front of a crowd as I read, vibrating like a tuning fork. I was also sick, of course, with little comfort except people telling me they loved the book, plus the awful power of conventional thin, white beauty, the only real social power my mother had ever been able to access, the power her mother had raised her to chase, and her mother before her, a power that may have endangered her in the end, when a man's fascination turned to violence. So I protected that form of beauty and ate small portions of the things I could eat and took endless mirror selfies, because I knew it would not last, and critiqued my hegemonic self-satisfaction in a distant sort of way and reveled in the resonance of our thin bodies, hers gone forever, mine defiant against the forces that took her. *Come and get me,* I thought. *I dare you.*

On Saltwater Taffy

Saltwater taffy contains the poignant sadness of a thing that is supposed to be happy and is never as happy as it's supposed to be, something that promises more enjoyment than it delivers. It brings to mind all the little towns north of Boston, their narrow streets swept clean by salt air, their ancient clapboard houses painted matte brown and blue, affixed with brass historic registry signs—charming set pieces that are enjoyable to visit as long as you suspend any awareness of colonial history. It conjures long walks near the heart-stoppingly cold water of the Maine ocean, gulls cawing overhead, wind shoving pieces

of hair behind your sunglasses, sun surreptitiously baking your shoulders. Saltwater taffy is your aunt taking you to the outlet malls or at least T.J. Maxx, zooming through terrifying greater Boston traffic as you do your best to keep your hand from the holy shit bar in her Jetta.

Even mediocre things have better and worse iterations. The best saltwater taffy is from a little store where you can hover over wooden bins and pick out the flavors yourself—this kind will be fresh and pliable, with a pleasing Silly Putty texture and a long, thin stretch. The lowest tier is a variety box bought in the gift shop of a historical museum or in a grocery store in a small town or at that T.J. Maxx, which is guaranteed to be stale, cemented to its wrappers.

Regardless of texture or flavor, saltwater taffy is always beautiful—presenting a range of nuanced pastels and bright, happy hues, from clover green to lilac to hunter orange, sometimes bicolored, sometimes bull's-eyed, sometimes swirled, and wrapped up in that semitransparent wax paper that casts a glowing shroud over it. But the taste never lives up: like the new clothes from your aunt and the shopping trip on which you obtain them, you want to like it, to be excited and pleased, but mostly you're bored, strangely disappointed by something you didn't ask for in the first place. The saltiness that could make things interesting never materializes (there's an apocryphal origin story about a seaside candy shop flood, but salt actually has nothing to do with taffy's manufacture), and the flavors are too subtle to make much of an impact, terribly disproportionate to the elegant dance of folding and stretching that goes into its making. You search for a good one, imperceptibly lowering your standards as you go, eventually comparing each piece only with the others, like straight women disillusioned by long years of dating, working by an internal vocabulary of pleasure that would be blown all to hell by the arrival of a Snickers, a Werther's Original, or a soft butch wielding a Hitachi.

Saltwater taffy was originally made in the 1880s on the Jersey Shore, which at the time was billed as a wholesome tourist trap for city dwellers eager to watch their kiddos scamper in the clean yellow sand, so different from the reality-TV Jersey that now dominates the national imagination, a jagged length of coastline decorated with mahogany spray tans, Ed Hardy caps, and glitter, like a cold Vegas. Cape Cod—which, it must be said, has its fair share of tribal tattoos and Caucasian dreadlocks—claimed the taffy at the turn of the twentieth century and anachronistically added it to its Olde New England identity. Variety boxes in the area are decorated with marine-blue line drawings of lighthouses and merchant ships, implying that the candy was enjoyed by kids with corn husk dolls and women in bonnet hats and wizened, salt-encrusted fishermen, providing a moment of sweet reprieve from their bitter Puritan existence. Now that I've learned that saltwater taffy is from Jersey, a give-no-fucks place in pursuit of speed and pleasure, and was actually never eaten by the joyless wretches who stared gloomily from my elementary school textbooks, brows furrowed beneath the weight of their ridiculous buckle hats, I might give it more of a chance. It's not good, but at least it's not Puritan. I might dive hopefully into a box the next time I see one, priming myself for a pleasure that won't materialize, biting energetically into an ahistorical candy of optimism.

On Tiger Pops

How wonderful to discover that a previously presumed-nameless thing has a name. These have long been, in my head, "those lollipops with the white stripe," but a quick search online identifies them. Tiger Pops. Name as exaggeration: they have only one white stripe, striping through two colors, each a different fruit flavor. They are visually appealing, the stripe almost a swirl. You can see where the different candy colors are poured, sometimes opaque, sometimes overlapping and transparently layered, a sweet Venn diagram. The colors are bright and cheery: vibrating orange with grass green, caramel

with deep teal, bright yellow with rosy pink. The pops are beautiful, and I've always found them delicious, even if you can't really determine which fruits are being represented in each one. They are fun, playful, the *o* in "Pops" a cartoon paw print. You never buy a Tiger Pop; they just appear, in grab bags and in bowls. I remember them floating around my junior high, but now schools must be too paranoid about health concerns and allergies to give them out.

But that was Texas, and maybe here in Texas they still do. Now that I've moved, once again, for a teaching job just north of Dallas, it occasionally occurs to me to compare my junior high experience with those of my college freshmen. After my adolescent West Texas years, I'd long remembered that "swats" involved getting taken to the principal's office and getting hit with a paddle, but when I related this to adults after moving back north, shipped from one aunt to another to finish high school, I was told that I must have been mistaken, my brain perhaps warped by my own recent traumas. As a white girl, I had not been paddled myself—the practice seemed reserved for Black and Brown boys with too much energy, a fact that I observed with discomfort but at the time had no language for—and so I was an unreliable narrator. A quick check online reveals that it is still legal to use corporal punishment in Texas schools—a proposed ban on the practice failed in 2023, the year of no-gender-affirming-care-for-youth, the year of no-diversity-initiatives-in-colleges, so I doubt administrators are too concerned about gluten or whatever other allergens might be present in the pops' production facility.

Tiger Pops are made by Colombina, the Colombian business that also makes Bon Bon Bums, gum-centered lollipops so beloved all across Latin America that their name has become a deonym, like Kleenex for a tissue or Xerox for a copy. It makes sense, now, why I don't remember ever seeing them when I returned to Maine, and I wonder how many other pleasures I've forgotten once divorced from the geography in which I experienced them.

I can conjure the feeling of eating a junior high Tiger Pop right now. Its wrapper is clear, just two pieces of plastic crimped together, showing off those beautiful colors. To open it, you can grab the top and pull the pop out by its stick, but this can be tricky; sometimes the stick detaches or gets pulled crookedly, which is, of course, dispiriting. I prefer to grab the wrapper right at its base, where it wraps around the stick, and then pull it up like a shade or a shirt. If you strip it just right, you'll have a little envelope where you can rest the pop if you need to take breaks.

Laying the flat pop on your tongue, you wonder why you ever eat round pops. It makes so much more sense this way, the candy and your tongue feeling similar in thickness, your saliva touching fully half of the sugary surface area. They're so easy to stick in your mouth and talk around, no big sphere in your cheek. They're more dignified. As a teen, you feel cooler while eating one, not so much like a child. There I am, fourteen, long blond hair and clear skin, baby doll shirt (although I hated that term—did it mean the wearer was a baby doll? Or that she still owned baby dolls and stole their shirts to show off her belly piercing?). I wore men's jeans and black boots, riding shotgun in my friend Nick's old Mustang, windows down, imagining the white stick in my mouth to be a cigarette, like those of the older friends who surrounded me, leaning toward forbidden substances but not in any rush, content, for that moment, with sugar.

On Haribo Goldbears

Although more of a chocolate kid, I always loved gummy bears, mostly for their form. I loved gnawing off their nubby ears in an innocent imitation of violence, pinching their backs so their little arms would open and close like a hand puppet's. Sadly, I grew up with Jelly Belly gummy bears, as Haribo wasn't yet as common in the United States as it is today. When I first had a Haribo bear it was a revelation, not chewy but slippery, each one a delicate little nugget that you could hold carefully between your teeth or destroy in one gentle clench. Haribo are not only softer than other gummies, but smoother, yielding swiftly to the tongue, wearing themselves featureless on the washboard roof of the mouth. Their only real competitor is the twelve-flavor variety pack of Albanese bears, which you must go out and try immediately.

Growing up, I wondered why this particular animal was the one most often gummied, although being from Maine, land of the shy, round black bear, I regularly had bears on the mind. And they were the perfect shape for eating, rounded, with some interesting features to play with, and, of course, cute. Why not honey flavor? I wonder now. Would it be too perverse to make a sweet of a bear flavored like his own favorite sweet?

Gummy bears do contain a trace of real violence. They were created by Haribo in 1922, modeled after the "dancing bears" then still exhibited in German town squares—soft animals, themselves violent when hungry, trained to entertain humans in the way we most desire, by imitating us. We force nature into our own image, a simulation of superiority. From at least the tenth century until the practice was widely

banned in the mid-twentieth, bear cubs were stolen from the forests and trained from youth, made to stand on hot metal plates, shifting their feet above growing fires while music played, until they needed no fire to associate music with pain, would "dance" as soon as they heard a melody. Whipped and chained and tamed to docility, they were considered a cute amusement at the country market, and Haribo's innovation— what cemented the founder's fortune—was taking preexisting gummy candies and shaping them into these appealing little animals. Gummies became less zoomorphic and more abstract and teddy-like over time, their limbs shortening into rounded stubs, but their original success was based on their cuteness, a suspect quality in this case.

In trying to connect my personal impressions to the wider world via research, even following a path as sweet as candy, I find violence again and again. Additionally: the dancing bear bans, ostensibly about animal cruelty, may have gained easy public support because the bears were often kept by the Roma, a feared and reviled group in many European countries. Promises to compensate the Roma for their livelihoods in the wake of these laws usually did not materialize. Additionally: Haribo claims not to have used forced prison labor in its Bonn factory during World War II, but the German parliament disagrees. And as late as 2017, the company had to stop using carnauba wax to gloss the bears when it was revealed that production of the wax was relying on the labor of enslaved people in Brazil. They are, of course, far from the only candy company with questionable labor practices, and the history of sugar is one of enslavement and pain, colonizers enriching themselves at the expense of human life. To this day, *cañeros* in the Dominican Republic and Argentina suffer appalling conditions to bring us sweetness, and Tony's Chocolonely (delicious, btw) is the only chocolate brand I know of that definitely ensures that its cocoa isn't made with child labor.

I want to believe joy doesn't require blinders. But some days it feels easy to conclude that there is no purely innocent pleasure, no matter how small, no corner of light untouched by darkness, that history is one long path strewn with blood. We oppress not only one another but all the other creatures. When I eat gummy bears, I spin them around and let them dance in my mouth before I swallow them whole.

On Sixlets

Sixlets are tiny spheres of chocolate, covered with a crunchy shell—like C- or D-grade M&M's in planetary form. They are multicolored, but their colors serve merely as decoration. They come in a row, in a clear plastic sleeve, and they're aggressively mediocre. The candy shell is thin and breaks to shards in a displeasing manner, and the chocolate, too, has

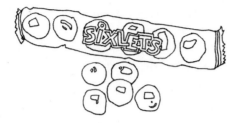

a thin consistency, turning watery when your saliva hits it. If you chew them, crunching them between your teeth, they disappear immediately, so quickly you can barely taste them.

Sixlets are a Halloween thing, mostly filler for the better candy. They're the bread in your meat loaf. Nobody prefers these over any other thing. They're cheap, surely, but then maybe it's the case that they allow people to give candy who couldn't otherwise. Think of being so broke that you can hardly afford candy for your own kid, then having to keep your house dark on Halloween night, ignoring the intrepid little ghouls who knock anyway. How sad to sit in the dark and hide, to not be able to contribute to the fun. Poverty is a million indignities, and we don't talk enough about the small sadnesses, the constant onslaught of them, all the alienation from ritual. The greatest privilege of money is belonging.

The chocolate in Sixlets is strange, described as "greasy" by multiple online reviewers. This feels like a cruel word for something many find enjoyable, something that sparks nostalgia for childhood, but, well. It does slide around on the tongue strangely. Turns out the filling is mixed with carob, adulterating the cacao-based chocolate with the crushed seedpod of another flowering tree.

Carob chips infect natural foods markets, posing as chocolate, and they wedge themselves into cookies unbeknownst to casual observers who, rushing through the hipster bakery line and pointing indiscriminately, are destined for disappointment when they get home. Carob became so popular among hippies and semi-hippies of the 1970s that, according to Jonathan Kauffman in *The New Yorker* in 2018, it "traumatized" the children of that time, "infiltrat[ing] . . . baking books as if it had been sent on a cointelpro mission to alienate the left's next generation." Did this work? Can we blame carob backlash for the decadent, death-drive Reaganism of the next decade, for Dubya, for Trump? How much progress has been held back by progressives' purity impulse? If we didn't fear our pleasures so much that we tried to hypnotize ourselves into thinking that this crumbly substance that tastes like stale cardboard could possibly measure up to chocolate, would we have universal health care by now? We may never know.

Anyone who tells you that carob tastes just like chocolate is not to be trusted; this is the sort of person who will insist that the pullout couch in their spare room, the one they've never slept on, is *so comfortable*. Spare yourself the pain and find better friends.

Carob comes from the Mediterranean, where there are countless better things to eat, and was originally animal feed. Only in times of famine and war was carob used as food for humans, calling to mind the substitution of chicory for coffee. The analogy is sound: in both cases you're losing caffeine, that electric spark in the mind. Caffeine is a drug, sure, and too much can make you crazy, and apparently it killed Balzac, but in maligning it, we forget how many novels and plays and paintings it has brought into the world. Did Proust not have tea with that madeleine?

If there's anything good to say about carob, it's that it lacks theobromine, the substance in chocolate that poisons dogs. "Theobromine" comes from Greek roots that translate to "food of the gods," and I suppose Pomeranians and Labradoodles simply aren't meant for it. Cats, lacking taste buds for sweetness, don't bother with chocolate, which as a cat person disturbs me deeply. But I suppose cats have their own gods, gods of fishes and oceans, gods of fields and field mice, gods that appear in heady catnip clouds. Cats don't eat chocolate, and we will never see the ghosts they chase when suddenly we find them leaping at empty air. Love is always mysterious.

On Mamba

Sometimes you try something new and it reinforces the very idea of trying something new. So with me and Mamba in the summer of 2020. Mamba is one of many candies that I never saw growing up but I'm familiar with from New York City bodegas. Somehow I'd gotten the impression that it was part of the pantheon of Mexican candies, but turns out it's German, distributed by Storck, which is perhaps more commonly associated with its hard caramel candy, Riesen. What's up with the Germans and excellent candy? They should lean into this harder, PR-wise. I would have loved to have seen Angela Merkel and Obama sharing a bag of Riesen.

So on a hot summer day in Brooklyn, one stolen from the onslaught of Covid, I got a package of Mamba. It's a long rectangle of cubes, like a Starburst pack, and I went in expecting some inferior version of that candy. I unwrapped a strawberry cube from its pleasingly slick wax-paper wrapper and popped it in my mouth. My taste buds jumped, spraying forth in that achy way that comes with surprise, and I bit into a texture unlike anything else I've eaten. The strawberry flavor was bright and fresh and the texture was like plastic, in the best way, clean and precise, chewy with no danger of getting stuck in the teeth. More chews extracted more juice, and revealed an odd longevity. They're half candy chew, half gum, Mamba, and although they do eventually break all the way down, you can chew them a long time and the flavor stays with you throughout. I stood there on Eastern Parkway in the sunshine, stopped among the joggers and kids on stand-up push scooters, all of us deciding we were safe, for the moment, and felt deep gratitude for this thing, this unexpected delight at the end of the world. And I laughed at myself, being that moved, feeling grateful for a mass-produced candy, but still, I looked at my hand, holding many more of these, in three more flavors I had yet to experience, and gratitude was what I felt. There is always something new to try. Despite histories of violence and ever-present threats, there is always a bit of light to be had. New York will always be there to return to, and candy will always bring joy.

Dark Chocolate Brown

On Mounds and Almond Joy

We all know the old jingle: "Sometimes you feel like a nut, sometimes you don't." One candy marketed by what the other one lacked. What was interesting here was that it wasn't a matter of sorting people by preference. Just: sometimes you wanted one thing, sometimes another—a sentiment that surely appealed to my nascent bisexual heart. Bonus points for a subconscious anti-stigmatizing attitude about mental illness. We're all a little nuts sometimes.

On Junior Mints

Junior Mints, the most candy of the mints, total perfection all around. First we have the box: a simple design, white background rhyming with the mint cream inside. Easy to open: you can slide your finger under its flap like a letter, cleanly separating the two panels so you can use the little semicircular tab to close it later, if you're at the movies and you don't finish before you head home. Slightly risky proposition, because if the box is under pressure, the little tab can slide out of its slot, and then you'll have smooshed Junior Mints in your bag for approximately the rest of your life.

This is a candy with good acoustics. Tilting the open box toward your cupped hand, you'll hear the mints shift down, making a Pavlovian *shhhh,* accented with the raindrop percussion of them tumbling against one another. Tilt faster for a louder *shhhh* and more tumble. This really should take its place with the woodblock and triangle in elementary school music rooms.

Eat some before the movie starts, while you're sitting and waiting with your friends, full of buzzy, chatty energy. Once the lights have gone down and you're cloaked in the communal hush of the story, you'll have to tilt more slowly, more quietly, to avoid disturbing others with the sound of your desire. This furtive element adds tension, making them more intimately delicious.

Junior Mints reveal the personality and style of the eater. I take them singly, placing each one on my tongue with thumb and forefinger. They collapse under the slightest pressure; it's almost impossible to taste the chocolate by itself. The mint cream dissipates into the cave of your mouth, blending with the chocolate and detonating a tiny, slow bomb of perfectly balanced flavor.

Some eat Junior Mints by the handful, like popcorn, filling a palm and then tossing them back. I suspect these are the same people who speed-walk through museum galleries, hardly really seeing a thing.

On York Peppermint Pattie

Oh, did my mother love these. One of the few candies I ever saw her get truly excited about. I can see her, holding a full-size neatly by its folded-back wrapper, shoulder just barely rolling forward, biting delicately into it like a kid enjoying a naughty pleasure, like someone finally getting something they'd been waiting for. I always thought her appreciation of them had a lot to do with Snoopy and Charlie Brown's buddy Peppermint Patty. She was a redhead, and Mom favored fellow redheads in a way that was completely loyal and completely adorable. She loved the royal Fergie, Anne of Green Gables, Reba McEntire. She had that outcast identity of all redheads who grew up in the 1970s, and it was important to her to hold a special place for redheads in the limelight, celebrating each as one of her own. Peppermint Patty was one of her favorites, a minor character on *Peanuts*, a kid who lived across town and mostly showed up in ensemble scenes. She wore, always, a green sort of rugby shirt and sandals that were clearly Birkenstocks, and when she spoke she was matter-of-fact and direct, with a husky voice. She was captain of the softball team, and her best friend was a devoted nerd named Marcie who called her "Sir." Peppermint Patty was gay, of course, despite Charles Schulz's denials, and I file her along with corduroy overalls and tap dance as things Mom loved, or urged me to love, that should have given me a clue that my mother wasn't entirely straight. In retrospect, maybe Mom really wanted me to know that she loved and accepted Peppermint Patty, maybe she loved her so conspicuously out of love for me.

Now I think back to the look that Mom would get on her face as her slightly crooked front teeth delicately cracked that dark chocolate shell, and it strikes me as even more cute. How refreshing that dense mint cream is, how decorous it feels—clean and sweet at once, an allowable indulgence, especially if no one understands how much you like it.

White

On White Chocolate

More a category than a specific candy, but I feel the need to clear up something here. Yes, white chocolate is chocolate. It contains cocoa butter and sugar and milk—all the things that make up regular chocolate, lacking only the solids from the bean, the part that brings the brown color. It usually also contains vanilla, which regular chocolate may or may not include. There are industry standards for these things, designated categories, and in most places white chocolate counts.

Most people who claim to hate white chocolate have a problem not of flavor but of definition. The idea of one thing claiming to be another unnerves them. The other factor in play here is the subconscious flavor expectation of the body, like when you grab your friend's Coke to take a sip and discover it's root beer. You might love root beer, but under these conditions, at least for a moment, it's disgusting. It makes sense that white chocolate is best as purely itself, and struggles when used as a substitute. I won't go near a white Kit Kat,

and the texture of those cookies-and-cream Hershey's Kisses creeps me out, the chocolate oily, the cookies exfoliating your tongue like dirt.

White chocolate suffers disproportionate vilification, especially considering that a lot of brown candy is merely masquerading as chocolate. Again, the operative ingredient is cocoa butter: if there's no cocoa butter present, what we have is "mockolate," slyly marketed as "chocolate candy" or "chocolate coating." This is similar to low-alcohol grape beverages labeled "wine product," which are good for a 2 a.m. booze run to CVS in a state with tight liquor laws, like New York, and not much else. Hershey's got into some mockolate trouble when it reformulated several candies in 2008 (not the flagship bar, which I detest for other reasons), substituting vegetable oil for cocoa butter to cut costs. This included, I'm sad to say, Milk Duds; the short-lived Kissables, tiny candy-coated kisses that died out quickly when consumers objected to the change in formula; and Whatchamacallit, which the alteration rendered even more abstract.

I don't need to point out that vegetable oil is a poor substitute for cocoa butter. While a given sparkling wine may be as good as or better than some champagnes, mockolate lacks cocoa butter's rich, creamy mouthfeel (a word that actually feels gross to say but cannot be avoided). These products really aren't chocolate. But are they candy? Of course. While a lot of processed food strays far from its origins, losing so much nutritional content that it can no longer really be considered food, candy needs only to be pleasurable, enjoyable, putting the lie to our contemporary obsession with authenticity. The Pure Food and Drug Act of 1906 even included a special confectionary clause, allowing for a looser definition of candy than of other food. Foods claiming to be coffee or bread or honey had to be the real thing, but candy was candy. Candy has only ever been extra, boon, bonus. The white chocolate haters are going about it all wrong.

White chocolate should be eaten in baking chips, straight from the bag, the creaminess of the cocoa butter coming through loud and clear, an unplanned surplus snack. A pantry supply turned into a delicacy. They melt almost as soon as you touch them, so don't tip them into your hand. If you commit past a moment of nibbling, you can pour a little mountain of them into a bowl or coffee cup and graze while staring out the window at trees turning their leaves over with the slow approach of rain. Keep a bag of them around, just for this. Pretend you're going to make macadamia nut cookies with them, and never get around to it.

On Candy Cigarettes

In Oklahoma, you can still get these at the gas station. They're not called "cigarettes," but we know what they are. We can recognize that fake Marlboro box, red with a sharp chevron down the front, the pack so pleasingly like the one your mother's boyfriend carried around, threw on the coffee table with a nonchalance you only hoped to grow into as you reached adulthood, strong and long-limbed, both attached to and carelessly chucking what you most needed and craved wherever you went. Of course, this box is slightly smaller. Kid-size.

There were two kinds of candy cigarettes. The first kind, more common in my 1980s Maine childhood, were hard sticks of pink gum wrapped in delicate paper just like a real cigarette, with a little tan filter printed on the end. You could clutch these tightly between first and middle finger, puffing and dragging away, breathing in the bubble gum scent and pretending that adult vices would be so sweet. You could stand mock-angrily in your backyard, surveying the grass with a hand on your hip and pulling dramatically with the other, exhaling with all the sharp irritation of an old-fashioned movie star, glaring into the middle distance and thinking of the lover who deserted her, the man who was in love with the sea, with the war, with the high, flat distances of the prairie.

Even as a child I always identified with the lover, the whore in satin and feathers, the stubborn loner fucking the priest, over the wife, the mother, the maiden demurely waiting to be selected. During the 1994 Winter Olympics, when I was twelve, I was firmly team Tonya. The bad girls had better outfits, spoke with more electricity, moved with more flow and energy, and if they were abandoned and miserable, at least they were free, and didn't have to do needlepoint on the settee in the evenings. They were the only women who could smoke, and they did, transforming fire into cloud with the force of their breath, the allure of their mouths stilling restless men, at least for a while.

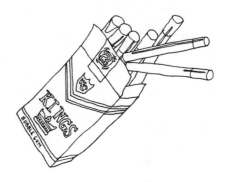

I spent a lot of time alone in the woods as a child, and this was the best place for fantasy, for practicing sex in my head. The woods, where no one could see me, was the perfect place to candy-smoke with an air of French ennui, with the anger of a motorcycle chick, with the refinement of the tomboy princess who learned sword fighting from a besotted male cousin. I craved privacy because I knew these performances made my mother uncomfortable. She rarely bought me candy cigarettes, understanding how easily emulation becomes practice. She perhaps felt guilty for smoking until I was seven, when she gave it up cold turkey after getting pneumonia. But her boyfriend, Dale, would insist candy cigarettes were harmless, and deep down she understood, she who had hitchhiked to visit her older boyfriend in juvenile detention when she was thirteen, the sweet girl, then good mom, who knew how to sneak away occasionally for a wild time. Candy cigarettes, then, were always an indulgence, a tacit recognition of that same simmering wildness in me, an admission that smoking was—let's admit it—sexy and cool.

I have gravitated toward sexy things for as long as I can remember. For my sixth birthday I desperately wanted a shiny red leather jacket. I somehow must have seen Michael Jackson's from the "Thriller" video, even though we didn't have cable, and so I wanted not only a sexy thing but a man's thing, the thing of a man whose power came from glamour. I was a year or two away from discovering a lifelong love of David Bowie.

That Christmas, I didn't get the jacket. Where would my mother have found such a thing in a child's size? She did, however, give me bright red suede boots. I think now of our rural malls, the Ames over in New Hampshire (no sales tax), its low ceilings traced by long fluorescent bulbs, the indoor-outdoor carpeting of its dressing rooms, strewn with straight pins and clear plastic clips; and the little store farther down, past the plastic ferns under a stark geometric skylight, the one that sold women's clothes for going out, teal satins and bugle bead embroidery and cropped acid-wash denim jackets. I would give anything to go shopping with her again. I would buy anything she thought looked good on me and wear it every day I could. I would buy her anything she wanted, no layaway.

I think of her scouring these places, perhaps a T.J. Maxx or two, thinking of my fervent red leather wish, wondering how she could translate it into what was at hand, in those pre-internet days, and finding those boots. I loved them the second I laid eyes on them. They were flat, with a pointed toe and a slouchy ankle shaft that—and this was the coolest part—you could roll down to make a cuff. Two boots in one. Soft as kittens. I wore them to death. I wore them on the playground and while doing homework at the kitchen table. I wore them to visit family and to sleepovers. No one could argue they were inappropriate—they were flat, after all, and in a child's size, although big when I got them, with room to grow—but they were bright red and sexy, there was no getting around it, and they were perfect. I candy-smoked in them with abandon, standing in our patchy backyard staring into the stand of cattails beyond, or sitting on the swings my father, Tom, had bought me during one of our rare visitation weekends, that we'd painted, splotchily, yellow and orange. Why I'd picked those colors, I have no idea, as they were my least favorite. I must have thought they'd be cheery, but I always imagine that swing set sallow against a gray, overcast sky, which would have suited the moodiness of my smoking, it's true. Smoking and thinking of my father, consciously or unconsciously, well into the Parliaments of my twenties.

The other kind of candy cigarette was a narrow, chalky white candy stick, no wrapper, with a bright red end. If you blew through these instead of sucking, you could sometimes see a tiny puff of sugar in the air. My mother showed me this, despite whatever anxieties she had about my future habits. It's true that sometimes you had to imagine the puff, but that was easy enough to do. Although they lacked the printed filter of the gum kind, the performance was more seamless—no awkwardly pausing to peel back the mouth-wetted paper, biting off gum that you then had to chew, the pinkness of which reminded you of your kid status, your little-girl-ness. Chewing gum while smoking was awkward, and not a thing you saw done by adults. With the candy stick, you just nipped the end when it started to disintegrate, dissolving it in your mouth, the thing neatly shortening like it was burning down. It had no flavor, really, nothing much to distract from the illusion. But if you gripped the stick too hard, it broke apart in your fingers. And you couldn't "pack" them, couldn't smack the end of the box against an open palm, like adults did, or they'd break into pieces.

You loved it when your mother's boyfriend packed his cigs, especially if he was doing something else at the same time, like talking to your mother. You could sense the anticipation of pleasure in the act, the practiced slaps, the smooth peel of the wrapper as he pulled the little red tab. Your smoking was all about anticipation, too—thinking ahead to the years in which you'd have, you then thought, complete freedom, when you'd be able to make any terrible decision you wanted, when you could be a beautiful, complicated mess, wearing any strange thing you liked, powerful in your little self-destructions, lighting tiny fires wherever you went.

On Mentos

I came late to Mentos; I never ate them as a kid. But I grew up on the commercials—the absurd situations culminating in a thumbs-up, the nothing-gets-in-my-way confidence of the eighties. The freshmaker/dealmaker always landing on their feet. The "hang in there" kitten, Mary Tyler Moore throwing her hat in the air in reruns, the sexily imperturbable girls in Robert Palmer's "Addicted to Love" video. In adulthood we would wear crowns of stiff hair above shoulder-pad armor while skipping from one shiny building to the next on thick sneakers—happy, efficient workers. No one would see us sweat, no one would see the moment when we pulled on the heels we hauled around in our bags, sighed, and got down to it.

I got straight A's, enrolled in the best college. Tests, papers, excellence, a social club that was a sorority in everything but name. Pearls at weekly meetings, mine a repurposed gift from my aunt Gwen, given to me on the day I stood in for my mother as maid of honor, six years after her death. Weekends were vodka, André sparkling wine, and bad pop music. Sundays, hangovers, one day out of seven vaporized in dehydrated pain.

Junior year, I broke free to study in Australia, still on scholarship. Beaches, heat, slowness. Trees that shed not their leaves but their bark, everything delightfully upside down. Not "Men-toes" but "Men-toss" when my boyfriend, Rhys— a tall, fair Australian biologist from a pristine island, a light-hearted nerd with a weakness for Americans—handed me one. We were on the beach, of course, bright white sand beneath our feet, greasy paper from destroyed fish and chips beside us. This was the beach where a great white would take down Rhys's friend, suddenly pulling him deep into the water and leaving no trace beneath the gorgeous blue surface, but that was a few years later. This day was bright and breezy, and I slipped the Mento into my mouth, realizing that I'd never tasted this thing that had loomed so large over my childhood, popping into every *Simpsons* or *Cosby Show* or *60 Minutes* commercial break. It was like you experienced them so many times throughout a day that you didn't need to actually go buy them; the ads were enough. After years of living stories, fantasies of insouciant freedom, I was finally out there.

A Mento is too big, awkwardly shaped, like a rugby ball. Something between a semi-flattened sphere and a fattened-up pastille. There's a slick outer layer that resists at first, your teeth sliding against it as though against a wave-smoothed pebble. Once that breaks down, dissolving sugar and mint into your mouth, you can bite. Then it's gummy, but not gum—it has a chewiness that yields, that doesn't spring back and persist. Still, you must tuck it into your molar and chaw, a blunt operation that contradicts the brisk nonchalance of the commercials. There on that beach on the other side of the world, I was happy to chomp, covered in ocean salt, hands laced with malt vinegar, hair wild, half-naked, smiling into the eyes of this boy I'd love forever, long after we parted. No pearls, no accomplishments, no striving, no perfection, other than a young mouth just fresh enough to kiss. The adult freedom we all imagined for ourselves as children—no school! no bedtime!—can prove elusive, a horizon point at which we never arrive. But that year was wide open. My body relaxes just thinking about it, and my mouth waters with the memory of mint.

On Swiss Miss Marshmallows

Are these a candy? Sure. They came in the packets of hot chocolate that Mom made for me after a day ice-skating on the pond, zipping past Dale's drilled fishing holes, imagining myself nailing triple axels to wild applause, gold medal imminent.

I'd trudge up the hill with Dale, him pulling a sled with the big ice auger on it, me wedging each step into the deeper snow on the side of the trail to avoid slipping, the blades of my skates digging into my puffy jacket, laces slung over my shoulder. We'd come in and Mom would smile brightly, so visibly pleased that I could tell even then. She'd help me off with my boots and the snow pants she insisted I wear (distinctly un-Olympian, so far from the tight, sparkly outfits I craved, bulking me up just like the turtlenecks she'd insist I wear under my Halloween costumes), then send me off to my room to change into dry clothes while she put a kettle on.

My room was an oasis of warmth—my stuffed animal family, my books, my Garfield comforter—and I would sit on my bed for a minute after I pulled on my velour sweat suit (bright red with purple accents) and just enjoy my little kingdom. Then I'd come out and sit at the kitchen counter as Mom slid a mug of hot water at me. She'd give me the packet of Swiss Miss and I'd shake the powder and marshmallows out into it. I've since learned that these are called, delightfully, marbits. They were smaller than a pinkie nail and

dissolved into tiny clouds lacing the brown surface, each a bright shot of sugar in the sip. Mom would lean her slender elbows on the counter and ask me about my day, using the soft voice that I inherited from her, one that forever prompts people to say "What?" and makes ordering a sandwich (or a Snickers) over a high deli counter nearly impossible, but which seemed, in the few years we had together, like our own private frequency.

On Life Savers Wint-O-Green Mints

Take a regular Life Saver, increase its diameter, make it opaque. Finally, a Life Saver you can savor. You can pretend you're having a mint, when really it's a candy—a virtuous indulgence. Just the right size to hold on the roof of your mouth while it dissolves. Or you can shove it into your cheek, where it will texturize the skin—this won't damage it, exactly, but when you flip it to the other side of your mouth, your tongue will meet slight roughness that wasn't there before. A deposit of sweetness? An injury? How often do we mistake one for the other?

In a 1988 *Peanuts* strip, our good friend Peppermint Patty and her partner, Marcie, get lost in a dark forest, and they find

their way home by the light of sparks emitted from chewing wintergreen candies. In the comic, Marcie explains triboluminescence, the process that creates light when you bust sugar's crystalline structure, proving that (1) we expected more from children in the eighties and (2) lesbians are the best people with whom to navigate a wilderness emergency.

On Valomilk

Buzzing around town the other day, I hit the plant shop, washed the car, and stopped into an Ace Hardware for WD-40 for the squeaky door that disturbs Preston's sleep when I get up earlier than he does. I was on a roll, leaning into my sunny suburban day, and must have been subconsciously aware that I was having the sort of Saturday that Dale had, over and over. Auto shop, hardware store, pick up a pizza on the way home. This Ace was large but sort of refreshingly understocked— empty spaces on shelves, clerks greeting me sleepily, lighting dim, none of the light-blasted, cavernous perfection of a Lowe's or a Home Depot. This was the sort of joint where you could mull over nails as long as you wanted without anyone bothering you. I wandered a little, open to impulse-purchase gadgets or unnecessary lifestyle items (Yeti mugs, leopard-print

duct tape, fancy silver Command hooks), but found, pleasantly, nothing to waste my money on. I grabbed my lube and went up to the register, where I found candy shelves full of old-fashioneds: they even had Teaberry gum. Mom had loved Teaberry, and it was rare even then, back in Maine in the 1980s. But the last time I bought it, I learned again that it loses its flavor immediately, each stick quickly turning to squeaky putty in your mouth. And the flavor is so delicate to begin with, barely perceptible. Teaberry is an evergreen bush, native to New England—it's also called wintergreen, but the gum flavor is a shadow of the industrial wintergreen flavoring we now enjoy. So as I stood there waiting, I scanned the Cow Tales and the 100 Grand and settled on Valomilk, which I'd seen before but had never eaten, attracted by its wonderfully old-fashioned packaging: white plastic wrapping with filigreed edges, "Sifers Valomilk" in soft, arcing font, like a simplified art nouveau sign, a drawing of a broken-apart cup leaking "flowing marshmallow."

Knowing how quickly flowing marshmallow would melt in the car, even in the air-conditioning, I ate the first one immediately. The outside is almost precisely the Reese's cup, just a little deeper, and when you pull the paper wrapping off, it makes the same tiny *tink-tink-tink* sound as the delicate chocolate edge releases from each crenellation.

The inside was flowing, as advertised, so I handled the cup carefully, tilting it up to keep the flow in. The marshmallow is nice, the liquidy sensation more pleasing than the usual airy fluff, with a barely detectable vanilla flavor. Dale might have liked these. He was, like Preston, pretty sweets-ambivalent, but he did occasionally like something simple, like M&M's or 3 Musketeers. I'd been running around all afternoon, compulsively spurred to blast through the to-do list, but now I took a deep breath and rolled down the windows, there in the sun-bleached, nearly empty hardware store parking lot. I opened up the second cup—*tink-tink-tink*—and took a tiny edge bite, removing a little door of chocolate and sucking some of the filling out. I let it melt there and imagined buying these at the gas station/bait shop with Dale on an early, crisp fall morning.

On Zero Bar

These haunt me. Covered in a white substance that's not exactly white chocolate—some kind of ganache, maybe? The company calls it fudge, but that's not how fudge works. Their base is almond nougat, stuffed with peanuts, with a layer of caramel above that. Visually, it's a photo negative of a Snickers, otherworldly and bright white, in a silver wrapper. "Zero" announces itself in seventies space-exploration font, the Z bold and angular, its bottom line extending under all the other letters, the cool blue of a 3D relief shadow making the whole name look like a decal on a hot rod. A mysterious, paler blue floats in the negative space of the letters, calling to mind the pure oxygen that would keep astronauts alive, or the crisp void of space itself.

As a kid, I'd eat these when Dale took me fishing, heading out early on a Saturday morning. It occurs to me now that Mom got to sleep in on those days, or sit on the deck in her robe and drink coffee while the northern sun gradually burned the fog out of the woods behind our house, and now I understand why she rarely came with us. First we'd head to an old

convenience store with creaky wood floors to get bait—little wriggly pink worms, yes, but mostly night crawlers, large dark reddish earthworms with a name I've never written before, and am now even more scared of. "Night crawler": what a dark and strange word to be used on all those bright, crisp mornings. Dale was perfectly at ease and clearly happy to have me along, and the old man behind the counter smiled down at me. Nothing could touch us, nothing could be too dark. Even the chocolate bars were shining bright. I always picked the Zero on fishing days, because it was a bit uncommon. It was also a ritual, eating them with Dale—the other place I remember getting them was at the auto body shop, where, in addition to the Runts vending machine, they had a few cardboard-box displays of candy bars for waiting customers. I'd grab one when Dale and I picked up or dropped off one or the other of his two Firebirds, which were on rotation at the shop.

Fishing mornings, though, we'd be in his little truck, a bright teal Isuzu. I can never find this exact model online, but a close match on a car nerd website shows me the interior: the vinyl-trimmed seats, the cloth accent panels on the doors. Blue, as Dale's truck must have been on the inside, with a large, skinny steering wheel and a stick shift like a little billiard ball floating up over the floor. The truck had a bench seat, and on the rare occasions Mom did come along, I could perch in the middle.

Heaven, being between them, safety enveloping me from either side. Even now I can feel them, Mom's red hair blowing onto my shoulder from the open window, the occasional diluted backdraft puff of the cigarette Dale held carefully out the window, the sweet citrus smell of the Armor All that made the dashboard shine.

But mostly it was just me and Dale, and that was special, too, as fishing was the time we were most commonly alone together. Special but not exactly rare, like the Zero. We'd get our bait and then drive to whatever fishing spot he sensed was most promising that day, on one of the dozen or so ponds and lakes in the area, nosing the truck down dirt roads or leaving it parked by some boulders on a causeway or on a soft dirt shoulder that didn't seem to be near anything much at all. I'd carry my little fishing pole with the Snoopy bobber, and he'd lug the rest of our gear—his pole, with an exposed, shiny black, technical reel; his tackle box, compartments full of mysterious, colorful objects, much like my grandmother's jewelry box; and a red-and-white Igloo cooler holding his beers, my orange sodas, sandwiches Mom had made. I might carry the crinkly brown paper bag with the plastic container of night crawlers and my Zero bar. We'd get ourselves set up on a sunny rock, or on a little patch of moss, and each time I was distracted by the glassy perfection of the lake, its surface shining silver and deep blue and bottle green, seeming almost to have a skin upon it, a protective, thicker layer. When we cast our lines out—the best feeling, that tension of windup, that well-timed release—the ripples were surprising and beautiful, radiating gently outward until they reached us onshore. By lunch I'd be so lulled by waiting, by talking quietly with Dale so our voices wouldn't unduly vibrate the water, I would have almost forgotten about the candy.

It's been twenty-seven years since I saw Dale. I hope that today, this very moment, around noon on the East Coast, where I know he still lives, he's on a lakeshore with his line in the water, standing in sunlight dappled by trees so tall they won't snag him. I hope a big bass is about to bite, that reeling him in will be smooth but not too easy, a dignified conversation between man and fish—that it will finally look up at Dale with a cold, shining eye and relent, and that later a pink sunset will fall down around the yard while Dale stands at the grill, thinking of the past, maybe thinking of that little blond kid with the Snoopy bobber, who loved those weird white candy bars.

On Needhams

These come from Maine, and have a cult-regional following. They're large, maybe an inch and a half squared, and of the "homemade" variety even when bought at the store. Handcrafted, we could say. Each Needham is a mounded square of coconut paste—shredded coconut blended into a metric fuck-ton of confectioners' sugar, so much that you can't imagine it'll even mix in—covered in a thick, solid coat of, usually, dark (not milk) chocolate. But the real kicker is the potato.

When you make them at home, or when your aunt does, in preparation for the annual Thanksgiving party at your other aunt's house (the one who doesn't mind cleaning up after the extended family, the one with the biggest TV and the rowdiest husband) or for the Christmas party at yet another aunt's house (this one does mind the mess but is better at deputizing the crew to clean), your first step is boiling or baking, then mashing, a potato. Plan to cook something for dinner later with potato on the side, because you won't use the whole thing, unless you're making dozens of these, which maybe you are, and why not. The potato acts as a base for the filling, for all that confectioners' sugar and finely shredded coconut. This makes them the most Maine of candies—all those third-generation potato famine Irish turning the old staple into a luxury, with, finally, no worries about having enough. In the end, the potato in a Needham is undetectable, its starchy blandness hiding under the coconut. But Needhams do have a notable denseness, a tightly packed solidity. When you bite into one, your teeth leave a clear mark, and the bits of coconut—the more finely shredded, the better—stick out of the cliff you've made, like crystals in a blasted mine. The taste is remarkable—the chocolate so thick it snaps when you bite it, the abundant, rough-grained sugar melting on your tongue like static, the coconut rehydrating in your mouth while you stand in the kitchen, laughing relatives behind you, staring out the above-the-sink window into the deep blue snow, night-black pines hovering above.

Although I feel I should most treasure homemade Needhams, the best ones were made by the Seavey's company. The Seavey's Needhams came in a plain white cardboard box, the company name stamped diagonally in black script, with a layer of wax paper inside, or else as extra-large singles occasionally found at the blessed checkout counter, in a bag-like plastic wrapping printed in orange and black. Were there lighthouses on the single-serve package? I hope not, but maybe. I'll forgive them—if we in Vacationland didn't appeal to the tourists, we'd all starve. And the Seavey's Needhams were perfection—the coconut bits perceptible but so finely shredded that "ground" might be a better description, so small that they never wedged between your teeth. In addition, I must confess that the Seavey's Needhams did not include potato and instead listed, among their four or so ingredients, some sort of harmless industrial emulsifier, which made them smoother. My preference for the store-bought over the home-made was consistent with my alien nature, a low-key betrayal manifesting in my lifelong desire to leave those woods for the city. I even preferred Potato Buds over real potatoes.

A box of Seavey's contained maybe sixteen candies, each a bit smaller than the homemade ones tend to be, one inch by one inch, and would last me approximately one day. You could get them at most grocery stores, for a while, and later, when production slowed, at Renys. They were a must at the Christmas season and made regular appearances year-round, and my aunt Carol and uncle Carroll (yes, matching names), when I lived with them in my high school years back in Maine, after my stern Texas aunt tired of me, did not fail to notice how much I enjoyed them. I would put three on a napkin, sitting in the recliner watching TV, and, moments later, get up for three more, and then three more. And so after I moved out—six months before graduation, under strained circumstances that were healed, surprisingly, by said move—Carol and Carroll made sure to have a box ready and waiting for me whenever I visited at holidays. They never made an announcement of this, but I always found a full box of Needhams when I looked in the cabinet, and there was always, too, an unopened two-liter of Orange Crush, my favorite. Sugar on sugar on sugar. I'd arrive in my little red car, always happy it had made the journey without incident, or else recovering from whatever breakdown it had presented, having driven the whole day, and be greeted either by their hugs in the waning sunlight of late afternoon or by the single yellow light they'd leave on over the stairs up to what had always been my room. I'd put my bags away, then peek in the fridge, then in the cabinet, and know I was still loved, that I had a sort of home to go to.

Seavey's doesn't exist anymore, the company having gone under years ago for reasons unknown. Another Maine company has stepped in to replace them, but their Needhams aren't as good. The coconut is even smoother, more a flavor than an ingredient, which makes them feel more corporate, despite the fact that they are probably made in the same small batches as before. And that white box is gone, and my uncle Carroll died a few years ago, and my aunt Carol no longer speaks to me. Back in 2014—yes, *before* I published a book about the family— I was permanently disinvited to Thanksgiving and Christmas, when, after my aunt asked me whom I was dating, I made the mistake of answering honestly and told her about a ballerina named Magda. We had been together for a year. This gayness was distasteful to both Car(r)ol(l)s, so distasteful that the sight of my face became something bitter, excluded from all invitations from that year onward, which gave me little reason to go back up there from New York City, where I'd settled. I never saw my uncle—a man whom I most often remember sitting on the couch teaching my little blue parakeet to say "Good little bird!"—again.

I no longer live in Maine, and I do not attend the family parties, but still, I keep meaning to make my own Needhams.

Years ago, I meant to make them for Patty, a former professor of mine from graduate school in New York. After I finished my coursework, she'd continued to serve as my mentor—the week I was heading into meetings with publishers about my first book, she told me: "If there's a bowl of candy on the table, eat that candy. You'll look more at ease, and feel more confident." We became friends, securing a close connection that soon shaded into the familial. She didn't step into my aunts' place, but she does love me in a sweetly supplemental way that I now can't do without. We need older people to love us, to make us feel anchored in the world.

Patty had always been drawn to Maine, so when the time came to retire, that's where she headed. Somehow, despite having a sweet tooth to rival mine, she had not heard of Needhams. I thought how sweet it would be if I introduced her to them before she even got there, a little pre-move celebration. I went to my cramped Brooklyn grocery store, found decent dark chocolate (Ghirardelli chips), pillowy bags of confectioners' sugar, shredded coconut. Grabbed a single potato. I obtained, shipped from the internet, food-grade paraffin, which you must add to the chocolate to create that snappy shell so the Needham doesn't immediately melt and fall apart in your hands. I considered getting special candy tools for the chocolate dipping but left them in my online cart. And then I never got around to making the Needhams at all.

They say it's the thought that counts, but people can't feel love from a thought they don't know about. I kept not finding the perfect day to perform this ritual of care and nostalgia. Patty moved north, and too soon it became silly to make and bring them to her when I visited, six or nine months into her life in Camden, when she'd long been able to get her own at the local Renys. I ate the chocolate chips eventually, keeping a tiny bowl of them on my desk to carry me through lonely writing hours, and the shredded coconut and confectioners' sugar stayed in the fridge so long I finally threw them out, well past their preservative-boosted expiration dates, but the paraffin remained for years, clear, plastic-looking beads representing my pure intentions, my impulse to do it right, my failure to make the gesture that would have brought delight to my friend, that would have made me feel like I was worthy of her love. I hid it from myself behind bottles of cooking wine and sriracha, occasionally catching a glimpse of the bag and thinking that maybe I could do something else with this special ingredient, something that would make someone else feel appreciated. But I never identified anyone who would want Needhams from my tiny kitchen, and I had no family parties to which I might bring them. The bag of paraffin moved farther back in the fridge. Only when I moved to Tulsa, years later, did I finally give up and throw it out.

Silver

On Hershey's Kisses

Lots of people eat candy, but only some people are candy people. The other night, I went to a gallery talk. It was a freshly hung show, featuring the work of two friends of mine. One creates large, photorealistic graphite-and-charcoal drawings, the other photos of abandoned public spaces, subtly shining prints full of bright colors and sharp angles. Their work stood together well, beautifully counterbalanced; the show was cohesive. So the huge, shallow wooden bowl of silver-wrapped Hershey's kisses on a low pedestal stood out. My new friend Emily announced that she was going to ask the gallery staff if it was a work of art or if we could eat them. She has long, witchy hair, dresses in vintage pants, is pursuing her PhD: not the sort of person I would expect to go out of her way to ask about candy. When she returned, she dived her long-fingered hand into the bowl, and I joined her in relief. Then we were rather stuck to that spot—we'd eat a kiss or two, take a couple of steps to look farther down the gallery wall, then immediately circle back for more, stuffing our pockets with wrappers. I noticed that, like me, she rolled each wrapper into a little ball before making it disappear.

Only later could I remember Félix González-Torres's name. I sent Emily a text about his candy sculptures, particularly *"Untitled" (Portrait of Ross in L.A.)*, which must be the most famous one, or maybe I only think so because of T Fleischmann's *Time Is the Thing a Body Moves Through*. Fleischmann's book is an academic essay about *"Untitled,"* interspersed with a contemporaneous account of their life in Brooklyn and on a queer communal farm down south. The sexual weaves into the intellectual, the visceral into the cerebral, the essay both supported and challenged by the life lived around its writing. The González-Torres work itself translates idea and memory into objects and weight: the piece consists of a pile of colorful hard candies, individually wrapped, nestled in the corner of a gallery and weighing approximately the same as Ross's body. It's a monument to a lover lost to AIDS, a sweet one we're encouraged to eat. The candy is replenished as the visitors gradually eat it. It's a sacrament in rainbow colors, one we give ourselves, reaching down and selecting with a slow hand. We take Ross into our bodies, dozens or hundreds of us, as Fleischmann's many loves and lovers take them in, are taken in. The sweetness is almost unbearable. What if a visitor launched a durational piece, taking and eating one piece after another, until the entire sculpture was gone, observer becoming artist? What would it mean to be overwhelmed to the point of sickness by someone's love for someone else?

Such an action would take ages, hours, days, because hard candy resists. Hershey's kisses, on the other hand, yield quickly. Kisses take only a moment, fleeting and transitory. You need quite a few to really add up to an experience worth savoring. They are just the right size and texture, can easily be chewed or melted, and the chocolate in them seems somehow better than the chocolate in the company's bars. I stood there with my new friend and we talked a little about the art, more about other things, the shining surface of the kisses imperceptibly lowering in the huge bowl. She mentioned that in college, each time she attended a session of one particularly dull course, she would eat two entire Cadbury Creme Eggs. Swoon.

When she dropped me off at my house, I leaned in and hugged her across the console. I kicked myself minutes later, lying on my bedroom floor, knowing from the remembered look in her eye that I could have kissed her, trading one warm kiss for all the silvery ones she'd obtained for us. I felt all the responsibility for the kisses that didn't happen, although there's no reason she couldn't have begun them. How do we come to these decisions? I wondered. Why wasn't I the one to ask the staff if we could eat the candy?

Black

On Black Licorice Jellybeans

Oh, you iconoclast, you. Look how you appreciate what everyone else casts aside. They're intimidated. More for you. You're happy over there alone, in the corner of the forest-green velvet sofa, pulling your dark treasures out of the crystal candy tray, one by one. Watching, watchful, in Margot Tenenbaum eyeliner.

*On Unnamed Scandinavian Candy
Eaten in San Pedro, Guatemala*

My best friend at the time, Mindy, is to blame for this. The summer in question, she'd been living in Guatemala for a

year or two, and I'd been in New York City. Years earlier, we'd lived in North Carolina, where we were neighbors on first one, then another quiet, leafy street. After traveling widely during her work vacations for a few years, she'd decided to leave the United States and the nine-to-five altogether. While I established my New York life, grinding my way through grad school and then trapezing from one gig to another, she enrolled in intensive Spanish language school and found herself an apartment overlooking Lake Atitlán. The town where she lived, San Pedro La Laguna, was full of people who'd come from elsewhere, were now of the lake but still known as "the Italians" or "the American" or, in the case of Mindy's friend's husband, "the Norwegian" (or maybe he was Finnish?). And then there were the occasional mestizo families—called ladino there—on vacation from the cities. All these visitors joined the Maya and Xinca population, which had become notably Catholic as a result of settler history.

When I visited Mindy in 2014, arriving in a little sky-blue boat and thumping over the waves while I gripped the side anxiously (I'm not a great swimmer), the town was an interesting, seemingly functional blend of backpackers, expats, tourists, and Indigenous people. At least that's how it looked from my limited perspective. Another little town on the lake, reachable by boat, specialized in yoga retreats. In another town, separated from San Pedro by dense forest, Hasidic Jews had settled, wearing their heavy black wool clothing even in the tropical heat. I'd traveled from my little apartment in Crown Heights, Brooklyn, where I lived two blocks from 770 Eastern Parkway, world headquarters of the Chabad-Lubavitch Hasidic movement, known the world over as simply "770." When we took a day trip and saw black fedoras, they made a weird sense to my eye, until they didn't. I crave a word for this sensation—when you encounter something in an unexpected context but at first don't truly see it, so accustomed is your eye to that image, until suddenly its contours snap into place. Like the moment when the 3D image in a Magic Eye poster finally reveals itself. Like when, six months into dating him, I finally noticed that my Colombian boyfriend, Camilo, whom I met in Australia, carried a Charlotte Hornets duffel bag.

Mindy's closest friend there was a sweet blond woman who'd built a beautiful house with her husband on the edge of town. She had dogs, Mindy said, to protect her from thieves. This struck me as paranoid, but it was and still is hard to separate truth from the confabulations of white anxiety.

A few days after I arrived, Mindy and I took a tuk-tuk as far as the driver was willing to go from town. We climbed up a little winding trail to the house of her friends, to welcome the husband back to town upon his return from a few weeks in his cold country. We ate lunch, some kind of soup the friend had made, and then, in a sunlit hallway, the husband handed us some candies to try. "Everyone eats these at home," he said. "Salted licorice."

I love licorice, anise, fennel, ouzo, sambuca. I love the clear astringent burn of it through my nostrils. I also love salt, that prick on the tongue. I was worldly enough to know that salt made chocolate better, and I always sprinkled my fruit with it, a habit I'd picked up in my southern years. So I was primed to like this item. As I felt the little hard nub of the candy through its now-forgotten wrapper, I told myself it might not be as good as I imagined, since it would be different in this texture, licorice-flavored but not chewy. I can't believe I was so innocent as to worry only about the texture.

Mindy and I put these things in our mouths at the same time, our faces immediately collapsing in disgust that was close to pain. *"Ohhh!"* we said, as well as we could around the little knob of sugar and God knows what. *"Ohhhhh!"* The husband laughed, proud of the strange flavor of his country, something that, yes, resembled licorice, or sassafras or Russian kvass or Moxie, something like roots extracted from a fermented bog. But this. This was one of the most offensive things I had yet tasted, or have since. Mindy pulled hers from her mouth in an instant, apologizing as the husband laughed harder. But I stuck with it, fascinated by how disgusting this candy was, by the fact that a candy could be so abhorrent. It was still a lump of sugar, after all, but as it melted, its fumes made my eyes water. "Wow," I kept saying. "Wow." I stood there, in a house on a hill overlooking three volcanoes and an expanse of flat blue sparkling water, in a country where I spoke none of the languages, sucking on this sulfurous chunk of hell's own stalactites, too disoriented and interested to know when to stop.

The night before, truth be told, I'd drunk sambuca with a Canadian girl who was on the run from some crime, as I slowly learned many expats were—a couple of Google searches usually confirmed that people weren't just making up interesting backstories. (The Hasidic group turned out to be extremely fringe, fleeing criminal charges in several other countries. They left the town on the lake years ago, chased out of the country altogether.) The Canadian had introduced me to an Australian guy named Steve-O, who convinced me (it took no convincing) to do cocaine with him in a bathroom, then took me to an apartment where I had sex with him and two other guys—one another Australian who looked like a slim, cuter Russell Brand, as if that could possibly be a thing, the other a round-faced farm boy, also Canadian, and Canadianly polite, even within the context of an orgy. I had no shame about the event, except that a little yellow street dog kept coming into the room and sniffing us on the bed, which felt unseemly, and also I remember how dirty the tiles in the room were, and also I kept having to grab the iPad and change the music when metal came on, because I could do this wild thing—have sex with three guys after not having sex for nine months because my heart was broken after leaving my partner of four years—but I would not do it to metal. Steve-O was a big, blokey guy with pillowy lips who kissed me like we were in love, those kisses the sugar in the whole experience, our connection weirdly compelling there in that seedy room.

So here I was, the next day, experiencing simultaneous disgust and sweetness once more. I enjoyed the shocked looks on my friends' faces as I kept at it—even the Norwegian didn't actually expect us to eat these things—until the moment when the solid wall of the candy cracked and out came a liquid center so revolting I collapsed at the waist, put my hand on the wall to brace myself. My mouth was flooded, attacked, filled with this salty, rank liquid, like mold and pus and the sticky substance you find on dive bar floors when you have to drag your hungover ass back there in the morning to retrieve the credit card you forgot the night before. This liquid center tasted like the nightmarish feeling of regret in the seconds right after you tell someone you love very deeply that you can't be with them anymore, the stomach drop that comes as you watch every muscle in their face clench in pain and surprise, like the first seconds of free fall in a bungee jump when you think you might die, when you desperately want to take it back and can't. It was, without a doubt, the grossest thing I have ever put in my mouth, an S&M candy experience with a Norwegian safe word I didn't know and couldn't have pronounced. I crunched through the rest of it as my friends laughed, rushing to the end, but my mouth held that taste for the rest of the day, through wine and more food, through toothpaste back at Mindy's apartment, through rum in the evening. I haven't quite forgiven that Norwegian, whatever his name was. Eating that candy is the only experience of that trip that I would undo, if I could.

On Anise Hard Candies

When it's rainy in Texas, the contrast can leave you gasping. Here, I've grown used to the glaring sunshine, the cement-radiant heat of our apartment building downtown, the dust devils in the parking lot. With the approach of winter, though, the dark days have started arriving. This morning was like a shade suddenly snapped down. I slept in, and in, hoping the sun would rise, but it never really did. For the rest of the day I could do nothing to bring the light back.

Now the dark is deepening, whatever light we had falling back down below the horizon. This is better. Dark is dark. Now I settle at my desk, and when I light a candle it means something. I find a little paper bag in the kitchen cupboard, pull out a deep red cellophane twist wrapper, put the brown cube in my mouth. It melts down fast, faster, sweetness mixed with something like the feeling of breathing in the forest. A concentrated herb on the tongue, not bitter but lightly medicinal. A tiny harmless echo of that hellish candy in San Pedro, of that sambuca night. It's a reminder: if you lean into a dark day, it can be healing, too.

Blue

On Gummy Sharks

These call to mind a Jonathan Taylor Thomas poster taped to the wall, opaque Scotch tape hugging its corners, crookedly tacked up in a fever of preteen lust. They're paper fortune tellers folded during recess, filled with your wildest dreams. They're water parks and reciprocal, one-day crushes on boys you wouldn't otherwise find that cute.

Almost the blue of pool water, these set the stage for the curaçao cocktails I drank in college, surrounded by other glowing young people who had also worked too hard to get there and now drank to be silly, to reach back and regain some childlike, carefree hours. The top of the shark—nicely articulated fin, curved tail, charismatic head—was this happy blue, soft and easy, while the underbelly was a slightly firmer solid white. I love the art in this, the careful replication of the animal's true colors.

The flavor was good—a mild sweetness level, probably meant to be blue raspberry, that flavor that purports to refer to something but is its own synthetic creation, neither rasp-

berry nor blueberry, a reference point only in the world of industrial food. I love the unapologetic fantasy in that, as I loved, unexpectedly, Vegas, for being just exactly itself. (I also love the person who tweeted that blue raspberry is "magical realism.")

There were great whites and hammerheads, bigger than other gummy animals, as though designed to eat them. They were wonderfully suited to the early-nineties revival of surfer culture. Delia's, PacSun, Wet Seal—we were flooded with girls in bikini tops and sun-faded sweats, boys in logo tees and pants made of boardshort material. In the mountains of western Maine, we wore shirts printed with vinyl sunsets and rainbow platform flip-flops deep into the winter months. Jack Johnson was coming for us soon.

Earlier, before, Mom would make bright blue Jell-O and add those gummy sharks, creating little single-serve oceans. The jiggle of the Jell-O combined with the chew of the gummy was a luxury of texture, spoon then fingers, and I dived in like I myself was the shark, sitting in the sunshine on the slab of cement steps in front of our house, while Mom sat in a lawn chair doing small handiwork chores to Pearl Jam's *Ten*. Although fair and freckled, she chased the sun, and loved to "lay out" in the three to five weeks that were actually warm in Maine back then, saving up the sun for the long fall and winter and the sharp-winded, muddy spring. We didn't have a pool, of course, but she owned at least five bathing suits: bandeau bikinis and a leopard-print one-piece and a tank suit with rainbow flames that she would pass down to me when I was tall enough. This in a place where we spent more hours shoveling snow each year than we did swimming. Her insistence on summer was part of her inherent hopefulness, and she kept more aloe on hand than sunblock. She could not have known how limited her days were, how perfect her approach. It has taken me a long time to adjust, to have faith that I'll be around long enough to need to protect myself.

When I think about her making those little shark pools, not for a holiday or my birthday but just any old day, I could cry. I could not have appreciated them enough then, so accustomed was I to her small, daily gestures of love. The least I can do, in her memory, is go to the beach because she cannot. To keep moving forward, to not just stay alive but to really live.

Orange

On Butterfinger

Butterfinger is Bart Simpson and skateboards, its bright orange insides mocking any concern about processed foods. It's flannels and cigarettes and muddy guitars, it's Eddie Vedder's voice crawling deliciously up the back of your neck. Butterfinger is getting pelted with dodge-balls, then walking home in the rain, throwing your wet jean jacket on a pile of cassette tapes on the floor. Butterfinger is bathroom earlobe piercings with an ice cube and a safety pin, tinting your hair red, the dye mottling your hands from fingertips to wrists, a pattern to stare at while grinding through worksheets at school on Monday morning, remembering the weekend's freedom, the sharp crack of decks on curbs, the sideways look from the older clerk when you bought your snacks, the warm press of your friend's knee on your own while you sat together and appeared to watch boys doing things. Butterfinger is the feeling in your mouth as you stare past those boys, the shattering texture of that bright orange taking all your attention, wedging far into your invincible molars, the chocolate melting fast under your fingerprints. It makes a noise like a styrofoam wafer, or insulation if you could bite it, and rains tiny shards of itself down onto the sun-warmed pavement. Butterfinger is a pleasure you can never get all of—some will always be left behind—but its compensation is that it stays with you, until you've eaten something else or fizzed it out with Dr Pepper or finally, in the open-window evening music of singing summer insects, brushed it out of your teeth after the anticlimax of coming home.

Butterfinger turned a masculine taunt into a positive virtue—to be called butterfingers on, say, the football field was to be emasculated and shamed. Butterfinger was a refutation of the basis of the insult, the idea that all boys must be athletically dominant, strong and capable. Butterfinger gave the finger to this: Who cared if someone didn't catch the ball, didn't win the game for home team and hometown, didn't provide vicarious excitement for grown men trapped in their own emotionally repressed lives of labor and drudge? Skater boys, Bart Simpson boys, slipped past all this, their gliding like a kind of freedom, their tricks and turns performed not for points but for pleasure, or at most the glory that comes from creating an artful moment more artfully than the next guy. No audience, no points, no schedule, no stats. Beck was a loser and we loved him. Slipping, dropping, falling down,

even spectacularly, was welcomed, each failure evidence of the heart to attempt, the vulnerability of not knowing whether you'd succeed.

What I mean to say is: Butterfinger is messy, and the last decade in which it was popular was messy, and both were messy in a way that I long for, that I wish I'd been ten years older for. Butterfinger was for boys, but it was one of those boy things that girls were claiming. Lines were blurring, fast. Everything good was smudged, underwater, oversize, a whip-lash reaction to the clean-lined, repressive, productive eighties. Cleaning it up wasn't the point; there was no neat way to eat a Butterfinger, and I appreciated that. I had been the kid who ate each dinner item in turn: all the peas, then all the potatoes, then all the meat. I cleaned up each section and then turned the plate, putting the next food at six o'clock. I lined up my stuffed animals and my shoes. I ordered my ice cream in a cup because I hated when it melted onto my hands. My Virgo mother, house so clean that after her death the investigators would note its bizarre lack of fingerprints, of course saw nothing amiss in these habits.

But Butterfinger was so messy it meant freedom from my obsessive ways. You bit into it and hoped for the best. You ate it outside, maybe, or over your other cupped hand, laughing with your friend while a little sugar-induced drool escaped along with the chocolate. It was like the houses of various friends to whom I would gravitate, where the parents barely cleaned, much less the kids. Houses full of clutter, clean laundry always piled on the couch waiting for someone to fold it, litter box always in need of scooping, where if you wanted a drink of water you first had to grab a glass out of the sink and wash it, so you ended up drinking from large measuring cups and old sippy cups with the top screwed off, out of loose-jointed laziness. These kids' beds were never made, and there was always interesting stuff in the detritus on their floors. My friend Jill's house was the best example of this. Her room was a beautiful, dirty nest—sparkly clothes on the floor, tape cases cracked by our steps, old postcards, an attached bathroom where the sink regularly grew mold. The utter chaos of the material that surrounded us allowed us to go further inside our messy selves, burrowing deeply into the music we listened to, then telling each other painful secrets long into the quiet of the nights. We were just pre-internet, at least in our houses, when knowledge itself felt more provisional, a collective thing made of memory and television and the occasional library book. There was more need to talk things out, to approximate, to know that you might never imbibe the whole story, that some of it would be left in tiny shatters on the ground. There was room for error and bad behavior if it didn't hurt anyone, or if it hurt only you. We never wondered why Butterfinger was so orange, or what the flavor was even supposed to be.

On Life Savers Creme Savers

A successful reimagining of a beloved candy form. They were larger than regular Life Savers, and the center was filled in. If you were sitting in one on the ocean, you could stay warmly lifted above the water, dry. The flavors were fruit and cream: the classic Strawberries & Creme, tasting like a turn-of-the-century idea of dessert; Orange & Creme, like a neat shot of Creamsicle; and Raspberries & Creme, smooth summer flavor

without the seeds. They were wonderfully creamy while still being a hard candy—undergoing a satisfying phase change as they dissolved. Sadly, they were discontinued in 2011; they've since been relaunched by Iconic Candy, whose mission is to resurrect lost candies. I admire their work, but the new ones don't taste the same. You can get them at Big Lots and various regional gift shops, but I wouldn't bother.

While they were here, these were a brilliant idea, a wonderful 1990s-synthetic interpretation of the simplest, most innocent snack. I was an adult before I ever poured heavy cream over real strawberries, a pleasure that is dependent on the quality of the berries. American produce being what it is, usually this isn't worth it, but it's transcendent when the berries are good—perhaps local, perhaps organic but not necessarily—and they are full of the sun and the wind, they've ripened and sugared themselves. You can boost lackluster strawberries with sugar—macerating, it's called, that sexy word—but then you'll crave shortcake and have to run out to the store again.

When I was little, tiny wild blueberries grew behind my grandmother's house along a dirt lane that led into the woods and out to nowhere. They were native bushes, not planted, the house being in a mountainous area. When Mom and I visited, we'd sometimes walk a few hundred yards along the lane and pick those berries, dropping them—*plunk, plunk, plunk*—into an old Cool Whip container. I loved how there would be one or two berries that were still hard white-green, rebels that didn't want to ripen with the others. When I ate one, it was bitter, more interesting but less sweet. The rest we washed in a colander, then put into a shallow bowl and poured 2 percent milk over, dusted with a little white sugar. Even though it wasn't chocolate, I loved this snack (a little meal, really, not sweet enough to be called dessert), because its flavor held the whole sunny afternoon, walking along next to Mom, following her gaze as she pointed out the best bushes, crouching low in the sandy dirt and threading my small hands through the scratchy branches, walking back in air that smelled not of berries but of the whole bush, a smell both sweet and wild. Even then, even as a small child, the activity and the food felt out of time; I felt a preemptive Nabokovian nostalgia, imagined myself a fairy princess wandering a long-gone kingdom, but now the housing development has extended down that little lane, and the blueberries have been plowed under to make way for bright green, ageless lawns, and Mom is gone, and my grandmother is gone, and Creme Savers, even, are gone, and I wouldn't know where to get good blueberries if you asked me.

On Gummy Orange Slices

It's July, and you're coming out of the pool. You're a little sunburned, a little hungry. You walk over to your lounge chair,

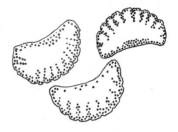

where you've wadded up your bag so your book doesn't get wet from kids doing cannonballs. You throw yourself down, the sun already pulling the water off you, starting to bake you again, and dig around for your orange slices. Eating them, your fingers get slightly sticky in the sunshine, the best kind of sticky, because the light melts the sticky down. You can suck it off your fingers, you can be messy, it's sunny and everyone's half-naked and it doesn't matter at all.

An orange is orange, and these are also but more so. Your teeth leave long scraping trails in these, and they're covered in grainy sugar that isn't sharp. You can continue eating them at your leisure, each one delicious but not compelling you, helpless, to the next. You can stop and put them away for a while, you can pick them back up for a second, you can share them without feeling torn between kindness and your own pleasure. And so they are abundant in their own way.

On Candy Corn

I enter this territory fearfully. Hating candy corn is some kind of American sport, the haters compelled by the contrast between what they deem its terrible flavor and its ubiquity in

the Halloween season, the defenders exaggerating its appeal. How to stake out my own position, how to avoid the politics of this thing and arrive at a personal truth?

I'll begin with an unassailable assertion: candy corn is happy. Its visual inspiration is the corn kernel, a deeply soothing image that reassures humans of the plenitude of this year's crop, calling to mind harvest festivals, happily hedonistic days celebrating the success of the year's work, final bright dances before the gray lid of winter snaps down, a winter adequately provided for, the stores of grain waiting to carry us through. Corn being indigenous to North America, romanticizing it is tricky—in truth, it means different things to different people, but corn usually means plenty. Candy corn is for Halloween, which of course is Samhain, a Celtic harvest celebration. It's also the night we leave our usual selves behind, a break in the work cycle when we can harmlessly flirt with spirits, safe behind our disguises.

Candy corn is one of those items that doesn't have to be as detailed as it is, with raised contours on its sides making it seem more like real corn, and the yellow-orange-white (or brown-and-orange) sections calling to mind heritage grains. It tastes nothing like corn, of course, the medium different from but texturally reminiscent of marzipan. It involves corn syrup (fittingly enough) and fondant and marshmallow, and the indestructible little kernels are made in a complex multi-step process. The candy industry calls it a mellowcreme—a beautiful word that, if popularized, would surely help its image. Now I sound like a defender, and I'm not interested in defending, as I think the people who love to hate candy corn are the sort who often pick the low-hanging fruit (or, in this case, vegetable) of controversy, so that they can feel interesting for going against the grain, and that's not a real controversy, not worth engaging in. Again, it's happy, fun, earnest in a way that you'd expect of a candy that hails from the 1880s. It was originally called Chicken Feed, which is adorable—of course, the haters wouldn't have the humility to accept being aligned with an animal in their snacking, wouldn't understand the fun.

Officially, the flavor is vanilla, and even though vanilla is usually not that compelling, once you start popping it into your mouth, you want more. The kernels combine chew and melt unlike any other candy, and they're small enough that you can chomp on one or throw a bunch back at once. They aren't for savoring; you can plunge ahead without rationing your pleasure. They're nice for tapering off the Halloween bender the first week of November.

Although long associated with Halloween, candy corn predates the holiday as we now understand it. Back in 1888, the night of All Hallows' Eve involved pranks like stealing wagon wheels and cozy indoor parties full of homemade treats. It wasn't until the 1940s that trick-or-treating became popular, and its origins are murky. The most common theory is that the holiday grew out of medieval Irish and Scottish traditions, particularly the practice of "souling," where children went door-to-door begging for "soul cakes" on November 1, following the Christian calendar but possibly influenced by pagan ritual. (Can I confess here how validating it is that my very own ancestors might be responsible for the ultimate candy holiday?) These practices would have been brought by immigrants to the United States, which has since exported the commercial version of Halloween back to Europe.

Candy companies started marketing their treats as Halloween favors in the 1950s and '60s, but it was only in the 1980s that they really caught on and started making holiday-specific treats, such as mellowcreme pumpkins, candy corn's more delicious cousin. In 1985, industry lobbyists sprinkled the Senate chamber with candy pumpkins during congressional hearings on daylight saving time, hoping that the period would be extended through October 31, giving children an extra hour of light for trick-or-treating and thus driving sales. They were unsuccessful under Reagan (that killjoy) but rejoiced in 2005 when DST was extended one week, through the first Sunday in November. Am I a little jealous of today's kids? Of course I am.

Candy corn has become a classic, and so is not to be messed with, or so I thought. Digging into the online candysphere, I find myself alternately skeptical and seduced by an overwhelming variety of options. There's Easter candy corn—cutely named "bunny corn"—and it's so beautiful, in pastel colors that strike the eye all the more for diverging from our visual expectation. There's Nerds candy corn, and there are recipes for candy corn everything, including candy corn macarons, courtesy of, of all places, Goop. But raspberry-lemonade candy corn? Blackberry cobbler? I'm not so sure about those. The Turkey Dinner variety bag, with green bean, roasted turkey, cranberry sauce, stuffing, apple pie, and coffee flavors, might be crazy enough to try out, even though I do not for the life of me understand why they wouldn't include a buttered corn or corn bread flavor. And I might allow pumpkin spice, even though I'm not generally on board with the epidemic of pumpkin spice–ification that begins around mid-September. But that's another thing people love to be lazily cranky about, and I can afford only so many.

On Circus Peanuts

I feel like I imagined these; they seem no more real than the witches that I could feel flying through the woods alongside the car as Mom drove us from house to house on Halloween. Pale orange with a sort of springy rind, inside they had the texture of stale fluffernutter. Did people throw these in bare? Did they have a wrapper? Did they fold them into little paper bags? Must have been bags. Yes, because you wouldn't know that these things were in your stash until you got home and poured it all out on the kitchen table for inspection, because it was the 1980s, stranger danger time, razor-blades-in-apples time. Mom and Dale wouldn't let me eat anything until they'd

inspected it for blades and drugs. Otherwise nonhysterical people, one of whom cultivated spiky green plants under hot clip lights in the basement and was "on disability" (guess which one), did they really think that the white-haired residents of the nursing home we hit up or the families with their lights on specifically to act as candy beacons in the night, those adults who dressed up just to be more fun as they opened their door again and again for hours to cute kids yelling the same sentence at them over and over, would slip sharp objects into chewy morsels—and, what, cocaine? into a Pixy stick?—just for laughs, even though they'd never see the effects? That they'd just sit there by the fire with their cocoa, thinking of all the kids who right that instant could be bleeding from the lip, crying and wishing they'd never taken a chance on what looks like a packing peanut someone scribbled over with a highlighter?

Their worry was understandable but misplaced. Although the story of lethally tainted Halloween candy is so powerful that hospitals still offer to x-ray children's hauls (I'm not a doctor, but exposing treats to any amount of radiation seems like a bad idea), "Halloween sadism" has been thoroughly debunked. Sociology and criminal justice professor Joel Best has spent decades fact-checking accounts of children harmed by Halloween candy. Of the hundreds of stories he's researched, Best found only one confirmed account of a kid harmed by a stranger's offering—a teen whose lip was pricked by a syringe slipped into some chocolate on Halloween 2000 as a dark prank.

The most famous Halloween candy sabotage dates to 1974, when eight-year-old Timothy O'Bryan died after eating a cyanide-laced Pixy stick. But it's not the story we've been trained to fear. Timothy was poisoned by his own father, Ronald, thereafter known as the Candy Man, for life insurance money, but before the investigation was over, the public had already been whipped into a frenzy about nefarious neighbors. Another story involved a child who ate his uncle's insufficiently hidden heroin stash and died. The family had sprinkled the drugs on the kid's candy after the fact to try to protect the careless uncle from consequences, which strikes me as both a terribly sad story of addiction and a concise illustration of how false stories of danger can perpetrate more falsehood.

The poison-candy stories all follow a similar pattern: the initial hysterical news item or Facebook post weighs more heavily on the public's psyche than the later, sober correction— if a correction draws media attention at all. Many of these stories are hoaxes perpetrated by kids or parents themselves, seeking attention or perhaps hoping to strengthen Halloween's eerie image. Humans have always privileged information that warns us of danger, crafting memorable stories to keep ourselves safe, and the Halloween poisoning story also acts as a convenient release valve for true anxieties (climate change, threats to human rights and bodily autonomy, pandemics, gun violence) that might otherwise overwhelm us. As Best says, "It's the greatest thing in the world you can be afraid of because you only have to be afraid of it for one night a year."

It's worth noting the speed with which this story took hold, the strength of our desire to believe the threat is coming from strangers, that the call is coming from outside the house. It's no coincidence that the height of the Halloween candy hysteria was also the peak of the Satanic Panic, a period in the 1980s when a truly ridiculous number of psychologists, law enforcement officers, judges, juries, and regular people believed that there was an active satanic network in the United States, operating out of daycare centers, that was sexually abusing children and sacrificing babies to the devil. The national conversation about childhood sexual abuse was brand-new, and the public wasn't ready to face the fact that most perpetrators weren't babysitters or strangers but people known to the victims—relatives or family friends or members of the clergy. So instead we collectively crafted this baroque myth.

My own experience would intersect with the since falsified "repressed memory" theory upon which the whole shaky edifice was based when I was relentlessly interrogated in the wake of my mother's murder, the police convinced that, just like those kids who'd suffered demonic horrors at daycares, my mind was hiding dark secrets that would help them solve the case. The cops were endlessly inventive, asking the same question over and over to try to get the answers they wanted. In one of these interviews, I said "I don't know" forty-two times in response to essentially the same query. The Satanic Panic kids were generally younger than I was, and under this pressure they created the stories the police needed. As we know, children can have very dark imaginations.

The stories of both satanic ritual abuse and Halloween sadism sent the same message: the nuclear family, the traditional domestic sphere, is the only true safe haven. Stray from the hearth and you risk nothing less than the death of innocents and the collapse of society. Mom was single, known to date men, the police told me. Surely that choice had led to her death, surely I could tell them which of the boyfriends had killed her, if I just remembered hard enough. The answer is: None of them. The answer is: Fuck you guys.

When I was a kid, the potential danger of Halloween candy struck me as an extension of its inherent creepiness: the night was for pushing up against the darkness, elaborately costumed and disguised, to see what the exploration could get you. It was about mystery, and mystery was as exciting as it was dangerous. Like a lot of New England kids raised in the ever-present shadow of the Salem witch trials, I had long been drawn to occult things, and would have believed in the Satanic Panic, too. It was only when real danger came to our doorstep that I started wondering what was true and what had been fear-mongering all along. The story that told us that all this candy could kill us was the same story that people later used to blame Mom for her own death, implying that she should never have pursued romance. Pleasure, especially pleasure you went out into the world to seize, was dangerous. But she was never not careful. She checked every single piece.

On Reese's Pieces

There are only a few circumstances under which rhyming is okay, and candy naming is one. Here we have a name that is a poem all on its own:

Reese's
Pieces

Evincing both internal rhyme and end rhyme, plus rhyming stresses, this candy's neat rhythm speaks to its sufficiency. We can also intuit a narrative: there was a person named Reese, there was a larger volume of candy that got pieced.

This linguistic density is reflected in the candy's tightly packed peanut butter cream, bordered and bounded by its firm shell. But the best is when a serious adult is in a rush, or under a spell of childlike anticipation, and calls them "Reesee's Peecees."

Reese's Pieces come in chocolate brown (but not chocolate), Halloween orange, and bright yellow—harvest colors that complement the peanut butter inside. I appreciate the outside matching the inside, even if we don't see it: a subtle harmony. Only an explorer, a connoisseur, is going to bite one in half (hard to do) and see the pale brown of the filling, but everyone who eats one will imagine the earthy tone of peanut butter. I can't eat them without thinking of M&M's, the reigning king of lenticular hard-shell candies, and so there's something wonderfully upstart about them, like a little sister or a weird cousin.

Sometimes Pieces crack in the package, creating clean lines, no crazed collapses, along which you can split one, put the exposed inside ledge of sugar against your tongue. Mostly they are whole, with the occasional flaw, a wobbly furrow in the oval, smoothed over like a dental filling. To get one that's slightly different is kind of exciting, a reminder that these otherwise perfect, mark-less little buttons are *made* somewhere and didn't just appear whole out of the sky, raining down like Skittles.

The peanut butter in Pieces is its own concoction—an unmistakable peanut butter flavor that's cyber-smooth, unrelated to anything you could spread on a sandwich. There comes a sharp spike of sugar along with the smoothness. It's possible to carefully crack and remove the outer coating from the nodule of cream inside, tucking the components into

opposite corners of your mouth so you can chomp up the shards, then dissolve that nub. A lot of work for a tiny reward, but its specificity is its own satisfaction, like digging the sweetest meat out of the tiny legs of a lobster.

Reese's hold up wonderfully to heat and humidity, remaining glossy and whole in most conditions. As a kid I'd make paths of them on the carpet, reenacting the magic of *E.T.*, acting as my own hungry, sweet alien. I was an only child. My mother was such a . . . not strict; let's say consistent . . . mom that it puzzles me that she let me do this, in a house with a cat, no less, who could have plopped his furry little butthole on any given spot. She must have known that she'd just vacuumed (she had always just vacuumed), or maybe she didn't consider it a threat. Parenting has become so much more mindful that I wonder if today she might have stopped me. Another thing that Mom as a mom today would never do: By the time I was eleven, mainly because I'd begged, she gave me a key to the house, let me get off the bus and wait the half hour or so before she came home from work, rather than sit in the after-school babysitting I hated. How I loved my little brass key, clipped to a ring inside my multicolored corduroy hippie backpack. How I loved that half hour (maybe an hour) of daily freedom, a rare slice of time that replicated the free-dom of all the adventuring kids in all the movies, where they figured it out on their own, with or without magic, with or without recognition, saving not only themselves but others, alone with their strange friends, backlit by a huge, bright moon.

On Chocolate Orange

I can't say I love the flavor of this. It's solid milk chocolate infused with an orange flavoring, maybe even real orange oil, or juice, I'm not sure. My love for the orange cream bonbons in the Whitman's Sampler box does not translate to these things. Here the orange flavor is too weak, reads more like an aftertaste, a shadow of a flavor, so that it impinges upon, more than enhances, the flavor of the chocolate. I find this tedious in the same way I find water with lemon tedious, the lemon juice leaking out weakly from the slice, greasy tendrils of sharp flavor interrupting the cold refreshment. Give me water

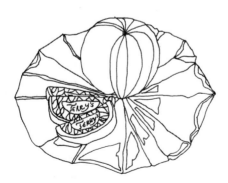

or give me lemonade. Bold orange filling or plain milk chocolate. Not these in-between, worst-of-both-worlds situations.

The chocolate orange's form, however, is genius. It's the size and shape of a real orange, the surface bumpy like a rind, containing twenty slender segments. It's somehow made so that it's one solid object until you break it apart to find that even the sides of the segments are realistically textured, each juice vesicle standing in relief. The suggested and best way to open a chocolate orange is to wrap your hand around it and smash it on a table. Purely satisfying, holiday-sanctioned destruction. Peel the metallic orange wrapper back and find the segments fallen apart, in a loose, blooming-onion arrangement from which you can pluck at your leisure. Beautiful. Superior to a real orange in its neatness and perfection, one of the best-presented candies on earth. No pith.

On Peach-O's

To contend with this candy, I must first think about its referent. Peaches themselves have always seemed overly pious, something too Holly Hobbie, Pollyanna, Annie-from-*Annie* about them. Peaches are cottage-core and hygge, Thomas Kinkade, Glamour Shots portraits, Precious Moments. The sexual peach emoji is the first sign of peaches having any sort of edge, plus of course Peaches the musician, but the fruit is so innocent it's covered in baby down, so precious it's almost never at the right level of ripeness, either hard as a baseball or mushy and half-rotten.

I have eaten peaches that were like heaven, standing over the sink because they were too juicy to handle responsibly elsewhere, feeling the syrup of them slide down my throat and thinking about kissing girls, glad I wasn't in public because each bite was an obscenity. But you can't make a gummy out of that. The candies are weirdly stretchy, an awkward size—too big to eat in one bite, but awkward to tear and gnash into smaller pieces. The flavor is industrial peach, super peach, like a drawing both accurate and lifeless, more aroma than anything. One is okay. A whole bag is perplexing.

But now my best lover loves them, and it's such a weird choice—so different from his fucking, which much more resembles the time-suspending sensation of devoting your mouth and cheeks to a real rare, perfect peach, an experience that has you bending and moaning and shutting your eyes against any distraction—that it's endearing. Next time I see them, I might give them another try.

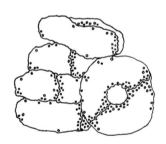

Pale Brown

On Tootsie Rolls

Tootsie Rolls have a texture all their own, sort of like taffy but both chewier and easier to bite. The second your teeth start to sink in, your mouth is ready, salivary glands spitting, almost embarrassingly eager. They're chewers, not melters. You can chomp them with abandon.

Tootsie Rolls have long come in a range of sizes, each with its own name. We've got Mini Bites and Midgees (until they're renamed, which I hope is soon) and Juniors and Snack Bars and Nostalgic Giant Bars and lord knows what else. This is before we even get to the non-chocolate flavors: Fruit Chews and Frooties and Vanilla Midgees. Why are Fruit Chews and Frooties two different products? Why is that fragrant vanilla made in only one size? Just as that owl will never lick all the way to the middle of the pop, we may never know the full range of this shape-shifter; we can only give thanks that the Tootsie Roll has generously adapted itself to every possible situation. The final mystery is, shockingly, just what flavor those brown ones even are. The company describes it as "a perfectly balanced

cocoa taste, lined with a subtle, fruit-flavored undertone." Who on earth has ever detected such a thing? They've been made from the same secret recipe since 1896, which also stipulates that the previous day's batch be mixed into each new one. So they're not only mysterious but perpetual.

For me, the whole Tootsie line is unfortunately tangled up with the name of my Texas aunt, who was at first kind and then cruel to me, treating me more harshly the closer we got, both spatially and emotionally. Her name was Loretta, but the family called her Tootsie. I knew her first as my mother's distant sister, who was in the army and stationed in Germany, a land of castles and war. She wrote me letters and sent me interesting coins from her travels around Europe (this was pre-euro), and I wrote her back, and she learned I was smart and good with words, which she appreciated. She had beautiful, steeply slanted handwriting and the most elaborately tangled signature I've ever seen. She was the only one in the family who had gone to college, attending Brigham Young before her military service. We were not at all Mormon, but her ex-husband was. Her biography was full of these apparently contradictory facts.

I met Tootsie once when I was four, then again the month before Mom died, when she was moving to Texas, where she'd been stationed after decades overseas. Just a few months later I would be sent to her for a visit that turned into a living arrangement, which turned into three years of walking on eggshells, terrified of her judgment. She was harsh even with strangers and would mock people behind their back for their silly femininity, or for being fat. At home she would intersperse her critiques with occasional, confounding kindness. One day when I was fourteen, she said that as soon as I made the choice to be sexually active, I should just let her know so we could go to the doctor and get me birth control. Another time, she cleaned my room for me when I was at the library during a busy school week. She was never sweet, but sometimes giving, sometimes calm and rational, and this made her angry outbursts all the more painful. Now when I eat a Tootsie Roll I think of her sisters, my mother plus the other four, laughing about how they'd given her such an inappropriate nickname. The eldest sister, a teenager when Loretta was born, peered down into the crib and saw the tiny baby there, wrapped up tightly in a blanket, and pronounced her "a little Tootsie Roll!" It's as though she made her personality in opposition to the sweetness expected of her. Later, I tried not to think of my family laughing about her known toughness and cruelty and then sending me to her. I suppose they were hoping for the best.

On Payday

What a wonder this thing is. A soft nougat-caramel center is covered in salty peanuts. That's it, that's all that's happening. Rare is the item that I think can't be improved by chocolate, but its absence here allows you to better appreciate the spiky contrast of salt and sweet, and the engineering: while it's true that some peanuts will pop off when you bite into it, that they hold to the bar at all without a jacket of chocolate is impressive. The peanuts are excellent, always with a good texture and flavor, much better than those tucked into Snickers or Baby Ruth. The salt is perfect, not at all puckery, a dusting, and the nougat-caramel (one ingredient, not two, as described on their website) is unique in candy; I can't think of anything else quite like it. I didn't even know it was a caramel until I researched what's really in this thing.

Payday has a good wrapper, too: white with orange print, block letters in sports font on a slight diagonal across an image of the bar itself. The word seems to come at you with the enthusiasm you'd have for the real thing: payday, yes! First of the month, or that blessed Friday afternoon. According to the brand's mythology, it was, in fact, payday at the plant the day they settled on the formula. It was 1932, the Depression— payday really meant something, and the bar, like many, would be marketed as a cheap meal replacement.

You can't properly enjoy a Payday unless your life has been such that payday really means something to you: the lights won't get turned off, you'll be able to go to the movies with your kid after all, you can repay your friend that twenty bucks you've owed her for too long. Payday is dignity and freedom

and ease, and these qualities infuse the bar itself: the sweet of available cash, the salt of knowing most of it is already earmarked toward survival. But every payday is an opportunity to forget for a while, to take a moment and get yourself something, to pause and rest and enjoy. My mother, who loved a Payday, was 2 to 5 percent more beautiful on payday, that every-other-Friday when the muscles in her jaw relaxed, when she shook out her curly hair and took me on an early evening drive, turning and turning aimlessly on back roads under cool canopies of trees, singing along to the radio as the light angled down orange into the evening, into the flush weekend.

On Brach's Milk Maid Royals

Dairy has long held connotations of pleasure. In "Milkmaids, Ploughmen, and Sex in Eighteenth-Century Britain," historian Robin Ganev examines the milkmaid and the plowboy as symbols of sexual virility, especially as contrasted with the impotent urban upper class and the effete nobility. The metaphors are obvious: plowboys marching stoutly between the legs of the plow, maids grasping long, warm teats in the

dark, sleepy hours of the morning. But a number of socio-
cultural factors established these two rural professions as the
sexiest. Those who labored outside were exposed to fresh air
and exercise, and thus had more health and vigor, and the
poor were seen as closer to the earth, more in touch with natural impulses. Commentators observed that families in the
countryside tended to have more children, while city dwellers
spent their energies in dissipation, attending balls and in-
dulging themselves in luxuries while avoiding marriage out of
concern for maintaining their own wealth. Ganev traces these
discourses (and their accompanying counter-discourses) in
medical literature, newspaper accounts, and, primarily, popular ballads, offering up lyrics such as "They're used so much
to ploughing their seed for to sow, / That under your apron it
is sure for to grow." Meanwhile, other ballads took the form of
anti-aristocratic erotica, censuring specific social betters who
had ill treated country lasses, or ridiculing the leisure class
for their perceived lack of sexual prowess. All this assures me
that the preference that Sophie and I share for, as she put it,
"broke hoes" (fit, promiscuous men without jobs) has real historical precedent. Preston is our very own "Cupid the Pretty
Ploughboy."

When German immigrant Emil J. Brach opened his candy
shop in Chicago in 1904, his first product was "Milk Maid
Caramels," their name subconsciously harkening back to
those ballads and stories wherein lovers wooed each other with
dairy products. In one, an especially generous lover offers a
country maid "milk, curds, cheesecake, and custards," and
milkmaids are frequently depicted offering their lads fresh,
warm milk, a soporific that surely leads to curling up in the
hayloft. And, of course, Brach was firmly positioned in an

American legacy of candy exchange as sexual advance, from men offering women boxes of "dainties" in the nineteenth century up through the Lindor hunk of today.

Departing from Ganev's study, we can look more deeply into medical history to appreciate British, Scottish, and Irish milkmaids' reputation for beauty and fair skin, their "peaches and cream" complexions. We now know that their exposure to cowpox rendered them immune to the much more dangerous smallpox, which not only killed thousands but marked survivors for life with deep pockmark scarring. Queen Elizabeth I herself had been thus deformed at the age of twenty-nine, leading her to adopt her characteristic thick white makeup, which was made with lead and may have contributed to her eventual mental decline and death. But milkmaids' faces remained naturally smooth and unmarked; cowpox is much less severe, and its pustules tend to concentrate at the site of contact, in this case the hands. Thus, the maids were uniquely beautiful, and their reputation as healthy and safe objects of desire has persisted, from the 1940s pinup "dairy queen" to Kate Moss clad in only a milk mustache in the "got milk?" ad campaign (although personally I find the one with a young, windblown Martha Stewart in overalls and barn coat to be much sexier). The association between milkmaids and sex wasn't confined to Anglo culture; in sixteenth-century Denmark, a church minister's mistress was known as a *mælkedeje* (milkmaid). The fact that there were so many of said mistresses that there was a special term for them makes me giggle.

Brach's Milk Maid Royals, a refinement of the company's original caramel, were never considered medicine, like lemon drops or Luden's, but the milkmaids for which they are named played a powerful part in medical history. Their smallpox immunity not only made them more beautiful, but indirectly saved millions of lives. In 1796, English doctor Edward Jenner developed the first modern vaccine by injecting the nine-year-old son of his gardener with pus from a cowpox sore on milkmaid Sarah Nelmes's hand. He also inoculated his eleven-month-old son (no record of how his wife reacted), and both children were soon found to be immune to smallpox. Jenner, like many white men throughout history, is given outsize credit, as the practice of rubbing smallpox pus into scratches on uninfected people (this is called variolation) predated his experiment by at least seven decades. His innovation seems to be in using not smallpox itself, but the safer cowpox. Before the injection, he already had a reputation in his medical society as "the cowpox bore," proving that those with the best ideas can sometimes be the most insufferable. In an apparent effort to cover up the fact that Jenner was only adapting a practice that he'd heard of when he was a young apprentice, the friend who wrote his posthumous biography conjured a story of a thirteen-year-old Jenner hearing a milkmaid boast of her untouchable beauty. This story was repeated as sexy med-school lore until it was debunked by Dr. Arthur Boylston in 2013. But it's true that the pus came from a milkmaid named Sarah, who was surely beautiful, as many milkmaids and many Sarahs are, and we unwittingly reference the story all the time, especially these past few years, as "vaccine" traces back to the Latin *vaccīnus:* "of or from a cow."

Brach's Milk Maid Royals won't save your life, but they'll help make it worth living. They are thin rolls of soft caramel, about the size of a pinkie, wrapped in jewel-toned foil wrappers. They are milkmaid soft, indenting easily when you pick them up, yielding swiftly to the teeth. Inside are various flavors of cream filling: chocolate, maple, vanilla, raspberry, orange, and butter rum, an honor roll of suitably old-fashioned tastes. You could eat these on a hayride and not be amiss. You could take them to the quilting bee. And I don't know why candy companies persist in making orange filling, since I am the only one who eats it. (Thanks, Brach's; thanks, Whitman's.)

I cannot find the story of how these were named, but the inverted syntax might be a clue. "Royals" as a noun, "milk maid" as the adjective: something precious and rare brought into existence through the labor of the proletariat, a high-class version of earthy pleasures, a luxury that's still lusty. Their production is industrial, divorced from any hint of rosy-cheeked girls rising with the early sun to coax nourishment from large, soft animals, although we're assured they are "real" caramel, made with milk. This pledge of authenticity raises more questions than it answers. Sometimes assurances backfire. Sometimes a declaration of love is more anxiety-provoking than anything.

On Tan M&M's

My plan for turning forty has always been to lean in. No self-consciousness about getting older, no worry about irrelevance, no suddenly scrutinizing the skin of my face. No procedures, no black humor, no talk of middle age. My concern has been more existential than physical or social: panic about how little time might be remaining, concern that I haven't used the past

four decades well enough, as though the lights are coming up in the bar and I'm just now realizing that I never got around to dancing. This is ridiculous. Anything could happen, of course, tragedy and death can come anytime, but it's likely I'll have lots of time left. I'm obsessed with time, so I've countered this anxiety with celebration. Three birthday parties for forty, and countless smaller meetups with friends.

I have much older friends, I have much younger friends, time doesn't actually mean anything, I tell myself. A laudable perspective that is periodically blown to hell by little rude awakenings, which are coming more and more frequently—the latest is the revelation that there are legal adults out there who have never eaten a tan M&M. Apparently, if you can remember these, you are "kinda old," according to *Bustle,* which purports to be a feminist website.

The proper way to eat M&M's, if you're a precise person and you're not in a car or some other conveyance, is to pour out the bag onto a dining room table and sort them by color. The proportion of colors will be different in every bag: life is always at least slightly surprising. In my childhood, M&M's were red, orange, yellow, brown, green, and tan. Yellow is my least favorite color, and I'd like to know why in almost every variety-of-colors candy, yellow is the most plentiful. Nobody likes yellow, so why is it so overrepresented? Are the factory workers plucking candies from the conveyor belt and choosing yellow the least often, winnowing down the other colors?

When I was little, I'd arrange my M&M's in colored blobs forming a clocklike semicircle with myself at six, then start eating, taking one (or two, or three, depending on relative supply) at a time from each color, then moving on to the next, so I had lasting variety throughout the session. Smell is famously part of taste, but not enough attention is given to flavor's visual aspect. Different colors prime the mind for different experiences (golden chicken telling us it's ready, bright purple mushrooms warning of psychedelic adventure or death), and so much of desire is about the tension between what we anticipate and what we get. A yellow M&M is fine, a placeholder at best. Brown is pure and direct—chocolate with no need to put on a colorful disguise. Orange is both optimistic and rich, red a shot of excitement, green fresh like a palate cleanser. This was just imagination, you'll say, but what's the difference between imagination and perception, really? Our bodies take in sensory information, which is meaningless until our brains interpret it, imagination and prediction always at work, stitching together the frames in the picture, calculating the speed of the object coming at us, figuring out who and what is safe. The real proof being the fact that the tan (or, as I thought of them, light brown, tan being such a flavorless word) M&M was the most delicious, a rare delicacy. There were always fewer than ten in the pack.

I saved the tans for last, eyeing them as I went, awaiting their nutty bite, like a more delicate version of the dark brown one. Some packs didn't have them at all, rendering the whole experience more quotidian. M&M's are a mundane candy in the first place. I'll admit it was smart to combine a chocolate with a hard candy (although any kid knows that M&M's do, in fact, melt in the heat of your hand, or the pocket of your favorite denim jacket, depositing a smeared rainbow of color). But the flavor is nothing special. The chocolate is a bit chalky, and the candy shell is merely functional, flavorless and brittle. Peanut M&M's are more satisfying, the texture adding interest, but still. M&M's are bland overall, the trail mix of candy, whether in trail mix or not, useful on the go, the peanut ones decent as a meal replacement on a busy day, but I've never craved M&M's, and I've never, not once, selected them from among the myriad options of a gas station or grocery store or drugstore candy aisle for an impulsive snack. They are culturally iconic, yes, and satisfying in the way that a serviceable (not favorite) pair of jeans is satisfying, or a solid (not favorite) pen is satisfying. I give them an A-minus at best. The M&M's characters have lasted ages, are perhaps one of the most durable ad campaigns, but they're not cute, not even interestingly uncute, and their lineage goes back to the California Raisins, the first personified food, complete with racist overtones.

I've previously said that M&M's were inspired by British Smarties, but that's not quite the right word. What happened was, Forrest Mars Sr. went to Europe in the 1930s and saw soldiers eating them in the Spanish Civil War, using them as portable, non-melting energy shots. He then ran home and copied them. The first run of M&M's were sold to the military, and the candy wasn't even available stateside until after the war. Was Mars glad when we dived into a major conflict right after he received his patent? Is America trauma-bonded to the M&M?

Tan M&M's replaced the original purple in 1949. A shame: purple is so fun. In 1995, when the time came for America to vote on a new M&M color, our options were blue, pink, and purple, and I was purple all the way. I didn't understand that we were replacing tan. I wasn't one of the thousands of Americans who called the 800 line and voted, overwhelmed by personal tragedy as I was, in that first year of missing Mom, but I love, now, that people did. What a simpler time, when people could so mobilize. Now every second of our lives is so optimized, so under pressure, so exhaustingly interconnected, that I can't imagine people taking the time. Gen-Z kids were deprived not only of the rare gem that was the tan M&M, but of a conception of adults who had a spare second in their day to care about something so wonderfully silly, to pick up the receiver of a landline phone and stand there tethered to the kitchen wall to vote on a candy color, of all the pressing concerns.

Some will disagree with my instructions for eating, arguing that surprise adds to pleasure, or that the colors don't mean anything, preferring to pull their candies from the bag as they go, but fifty or so surprises will dull, and who eats without using their eyes, and personally I can't fully commit to enjoyment if I know I could be eating my last red one and not even know it. Beneath any peaceful moment is the panic that I could be nearing its end.

On Werther's Original

Perhaps the hard candy with the most stamina, these are perfect for summer days spent reading romances on the top bunk, holding one in your mouth for a chapter or so, then reaching to the pile you've stashed beside you for the next. Throw the golden wrappers on the floor for your cat to play with, kick through them on the way to the bathroom, scoop them up like treasure and drop them in the trash can on your way back to your little cave. Good for winter, too, seeming to exude their own warmth as you wait for the bus, breathing out your little cloud of fog. Next year, when you dig out your jacket from the back closet, you might find one you missed, a gift from your past self.

Werther is both the German town in which these were conceived and the protagonist of Goethe's *The Sorrows of Young Werther,* an icon of unrequited love who, bereft, ends his own life. Half a century later, Frankenstein's monster uses the novel to teach himself to read, and sees in it an echo of his own pain at being rejected by his creator and the rest of humanity. And in *A Lover's Discourse,* Roland Barthes uses *Werther* as a source text for his explication of the roles of the lover and the beloved. With more resignation than bitterness, he writes, "The lover's fatal identity is precisely this: I am the one who waits." Werther ended his life when he could wait no longer.

The shape of these is perfect: a fat oval lozenge, flat on one side and rounded, with a little crater in the middle, on the other. A shape that gives your tongue something to explore as you work it down. The flavor is not quite caramel, as you can't really taste caramel without its texture, and they're so milky, something more like dulce de leche. They are incredibly rich, but never enough. Each one takes so long to eat that when it finally disappears, I experience a sort of loneliness. The Japanese word for this sensation is *kuchisabishii*—"lonely mouth." Often I eat the next one not because I want it but to address this desolate lack.

To decide to stop eating Werther's, when there are still some to be had, is to accept what Werther could not, that having the beloved actually solves nothing, that this lack can never be truly satisfied. When my house is emptied of them, I become a candy lover. I wait.

On See's Lollipops

These enjoy what every writer desires: prime airport placement. If you know them, that's where you've seen them, or else you're from California.

I discovered these through my ex-boyfriend Ari, who grew up in Long Beach. After dating for three weeks, we flew together cross-country to see his best friend get married. Ari was best man. We had actually met because the same woman dated us, one after the other. (She dumped us both, not yet over her ex—thank you, Jackie.) I remember sitting in his car in North Carolina as he dropped me off at my place one night, and him asking me, "Would it be crazy to ask you . . . ?"

Of course I wanted to attend a wedding with this sweet man, the one who kissed me so softly, the one who was so smart and thought I was, too, the one with the kind eyes and gentle hands. We were so sure of each other from the start, at least at the start. How long "the start" lasted, I am still trying to determine.

I got the couple days off work and we bought plane tickets, seats side by side. I loved seeing our names together in the email. I had been to California only to run through LAX on my way to Australia. Two nights before we left, we went out dancing, and a too exuberant piggyback ride, or attempt at one, ended with my upper lip torn and swollen, my front teeth forever delicately crazed although, in the end, not broken. My face was still oozing as we moved through the TSA line, which made me feel vulnerable, like a troublemaker who might get pulled aside. I didn't get pulled aside. Mostly we thought it was funny. He made me feel so beautiful that I didn't care that my face was a little damaged when I met his younger sister, his bestie, the bride, the groom, and his ex, the woman he'd been with for four or so years, traveled Europe with, been engaged to, broken up with only about a year before, the woman who, it turned out, would be officiating the wedding. When did I learn she would be central to this event? My complete lack of memory here reveals how confident I was in this match, how completely secure.

Ari had lived in California so recently that his former roommate still lived in their apartment, and we stayed in his former bedroom. He didn't touch me there. Barely kissed me. He must have felt weighted with the memory of his nights there with her, but I can only guess, because when I gently tried to approach him, asked how he was feeling, when I asked him to at least acknowledge the sudden distance between us on this romantic trip, he acted as though nothing was wrong. I didn't push it. How many dates had we even been on? Five?

The wedding was in a beautiful outdoor space, with fountains and palm trees, a tiled courtyard in the middle of some sort of commercial complex, and there was a See's store nearby. Ari pointed it out and told me that his father had been the architect. "For that store?" I asked. "All the stores," he said. I could not claim that this indication of relative wealth was something he'd been hiding, so early on, but I had trouble wrapping my head around what it could mean to have a father who designed a chain of stores that ran up and down the California coast, a design that would be replicated nationwide in the coming years. I wasn't even sure what it meant technically. So he was responsible for the minimalist black-and-white design of the interior, the airy sophistication, so different from the multicolored fantasy of most candy shops? Or did he have something to do with the pitch of each roof, the shape of each entrance? That world was so far from mine, I didn't even know what questions to ask. Ari didn't explain, another silence in the face of, probably, a larger reaction than he'd expected. His family was broken in many ways, and he didn't want me to get the wrong idea, think that his upbringing had been easy. I didn't think that. But.

We didn't go into the store, hustled along to the venue. We'd arrived early, because the ex was panicking. The wedding was in a couple of hours and she hadn't yet written her script. She was choking, and needed Ari's help. He was the writer, and she knew he knew about love. I left them by a fountain as I wandered among the palms, hoping I wouldn't get sunburned before the ceremony began. I wore a satin dress, tight and shirred, in deep magenta, and knew I looked good, despite my damaged face. She wore an empire-waist sundress, straight brown hair, clear innocence, glasses. She sweetly greeted me, this stranger in very high heels with a face marked by her own recklessness.

I got too drunk at the wedding, got angry about all my old wounds. It was my way of making sure he knew just how damaged I thought myself to be. I did it in front of his sister, nineteen and stunning, preternaturally mature and unfazed by me in a way that said a lot about the family's dysfunctions. He should have left me when we got back to North Carolina, but he didn't. He kept loving me. He loved me through our move to Louisiana three months later, when he began his PhD program, and he loved me through all the months when he had no desire for me, and he loved me through all the nights I came home Louisiana drunk, crashing into the bed mere hours before he had to get up and go to class. He loved me through my talking endlessly about my roller derby team, through my barely ever cooking or cleaning, through my refusal to fly to Europe with him when he had grant money for a project and invited me along. He loved me through my sleeping with another man, when I wanted an escape hatch from all that loving, all that near-silent loving, all those nights of curling up like twins in our sexless bed. He loved me through my not wanting to make it better. He loved me as I left, sleeping on friends' couches for the handful of months before I moved to New York to become a writer so I could simultaneously thank and betray him by writing about us.

See's shops are in nearly every airport. Sometimes I step into those clean, stripped-down oases, take a break from the hectic rush of the terminal. I always get the lollipops, a sort of flavored super-hard caramel wedge on a stick: coffee, vanilla, chocolate, butterscotch. They last ages, almost an hour if you're gentle with them.

Milk Chocolate Brown

On Rolos

This is the perfect candy for the car. A cylinder of chocolate-covered caramel nuggets, wrapped up in gold foil, covered in a neat paper sleeve, just made for adventuring. You don't need to bite them, can instead dole them out to yourself one by one, pinching each out of the package and slipping it into your mouth as you barrel down the highway. You don't have to worry about them melting in your grip, about cleaning up; there are no crumbs or drips to brush off your lap, no driving distractions. Choosing Rolos could save your life, the shredded gold gathering in the pocket of your door testament to the fact that there's still work for you to do, here on earth, where you also get to enjoy the most intensely sweet and soft caramel. It sticks in your teeth just long enough for you to pull it out with the suction of your mouth—decadent, then clean.

Rolos are the candy that, when pressed, I will designate as my favorite, but here's a secret you may already know: I'm lying. When people ask me—and they often ask me—what my favorite candy is, a wave of consternation flows through me.

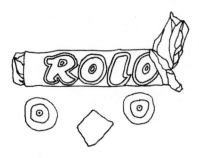

The very premise strikes me as ridiculous. It's impossible to crown a single candy as the best. Is it perhaps even rude of people to ask, I wonder, like asking a parent which is their favorite child or—more relevant in my case—asking a polyamorous person whom they would choose if they had to?

I follow the Swedish model, summed up on the website of Sockerbit, a leading Scandinavian candy dealer specializing in the pick-and-mix delivery model so popular over there: "It all depends on how we feel, our mood, the weather... You could say that each person's candy bag reflects the state of mind of that person." The Swedish know what they're talking about; they eat more candy per capita than any other country (thirty pounds per year, which strikes me as perfectly rational) and observe a weekly ritual called *lördagsgodis*—"Saturday candy"—a socially sanctioned day of indulgence on which everyone heads to their local shop and gets as much as they want, in whatever variety strikes their fancy.

So I go into my spiel. I say it depends. Maybe I just ate dinner, and the entrée might suggest a particular sort of follow-up. Maybe I'm in a quiet place and need to consider wrapper noise. Maybe I'm wearing my favorite pants, sitting on a lawn watching a band in the summer heat, so I need to eat something clean and neat, like a gummy. Often this candy philosophizing leaves my listener, and maybe my reader, with a strained, expectant look on their face. *Okay,* they seem to say, or do actually say, *but what's your* favorite? *Surely you have one.*

I'm coming around to the idea that it's not the question that's ridiculous, but my interpretation. Of course I can't designate what's best. What these people are really asking me is: *What kind of person are you?* So that they can figure out if we'll understand each other. Do we share a favorite? Given a whole world of options, would we reach for similar pleasures? Or would my favorite disgust them, and thus give them something to think about, pique their curiosity? To refuse to answer is to shove the questioner away, deny connection. And so I'll cave and say: Rolos. The sweetest of the sweet, the candiest of the candy. Portable, peripatetic. Concerned about not leaving a mess. Not too fancy, but wrapped up in a little gold, just for fun.

On Cadbury Creme Eggs

Mom would get these for me in the Easter season, when they sat in a wicker basket on the checkout counter upstairs at Renys, the discount store in the center of our little Maine town. Renys is an institution in the state, barely known to outsiders and far more culturally important than lighthouses or leaf peeping. It's the retail end of the line, like T.J. Maxx or Marshalls (both also beloved by New Englanders), where you can find Carhartts or Barbies or Jessica Simpson perfume or woven Guatemalan scarves at steep discounts, and part of the fun is showing up and seeing what's there, what's washed ashore from the cities, from civilization, down there, to the west.

In the year after 9/11, I read a *New York Times* article about small-town Mainers grocery-shopping in Gucci and Prada, inventory that had been salvaged from a huge store near the towers and pushed back out through the valve of an unnamed discount store chain. I was sure it was Renys. These people had made Renys finds for the ages, whether or not they'd ever heard of John Galliano, and I hoped they knew that their twenty-dollar tops retailed for four hundred. I hoped the original retail prices were still on the printed tags, legible underneath the bright orange tabs from the sticker gun, because another part of the fun of Renys was feeling like we'd gotten one over on them, those faceless dupes who paid retail, as though we were winning capitalism, somehow exempt from it while still enjoying its spoils. And I hoped they would never know that those tops and dresses came from the site of a massacre. That's one version of the story. The *Times* article, like many stories about Maine, wasn't for us, or at least not for those who still lived there. It was probably exactly for me, a small-town transplant to New York.

The weird blip of the Prada moment was followed by a steadily increasing volume of Renys items that were, in fact, full price, if not luxury (I hope the Creme Eggs weren't the start of this), and now you have to do more digging to find, say, steeply discounted L.L.Bean fleece-lined hoodies with an errant stitch you'll never see or care about. The stock has become less weird, more mainstream, but Mainers hold on to their love of the place. My Renys days were not only pre-Prada but pre-NAFTA (which would soon close down the Shoe Shop, where Mom had worked), before globalization became a subject of popular debate, when you didn't presume, as we do now in the Amazon age, that you could think up desires and go out and obtain whatever you wanted, when instead you canvassed the available items and, like Marie Kondo, meditated upon each one to see what might bring you joy. Cadbury Creme Eggs were available only during Easter, and back then they were the only Cadbury product Americans had regular access to. I wouldn't discover Dairy Milk and Flake until my junior year of college in Australia, when I felt duped and swore never to eat a waxy shingle of Hershey bar ever again.

Cadbury Creme Egg season was announced by their commercial, an incredibly soft-looking bunny incubating a pile of the eggs, with a chicken-like *bawk-bawk-bawk* voiceover—a calm murmur of chicken voice, y'know, the sort that a chocolate-egg-laying bunny would emit. To my kid mind it all made sense: this wasn't the Easter Bunny, the creepy anthropomorph who walked around on his hind legs and, for some reason, had a Santa-like desire for kids to sit on his furry lap. No, she was just a bunny, a soft, natural animal who happened to have the magical power of laying chocolate eggs filled with knee-weakening cream, runny like soft-boiled eggs are, opaque white streaked with yellow, the touch of verisimilitude unnecessary and therefore a kind of corporate generosity.

Cadbury had made not only a candy but a whole story, a subplot to Easter, which in my house never had anything to do with an assassinated messiah coming back to life. You could participate in the Cadbury story by eating the eggs, hoping that someday you might pet an animal that soft, hear a bunny cluck and know that the world was more magical than they wanted you to think, that joy might always be lurking where you least expect it, that at any moment you might be wearing Prada and not even have noticed, that there was no escaping how complicated and dangerous and violent your country was, but sometimes there would be these bright moments, seasonal dispatches from elsewhere, elsewheres you would someday visit, even live in, where it turned out that the geniuses who made this egg had made dozens of other candies, and you'd never known, and now you could eat them all.

On Caramello

A narrow bar in a royal-purple wrapper, Caramello is another candy that reaches for an elegance above its station. Popular in the nineties, they're now a little hard to find, but not rare. Walgreens has them, but not CVS. That you have to intentionally obtain one, rather than grab it from the lower shelf at any cash register where you might find yourself, adds to its allure.

I always loved Caramello, as I love most caramel things. It's a quick-release version of Rolos. And I loved asking for it, saying its name, flowing like the caramel within it. *Cara-mello*, naturally euphonic, like "cellar door."

On Snickers

The über candy bar. Look at the texture on the top of this chocolate—the sensual waves of its pouring, frozen and waiting for your eye, subliminally referencing that moment of melty abundance and sparking your desire, its ridges and valleys calling to mind nothing less than the surface of a realistic dildo. In 2022 there was an internet rumor that the Snickers veins would be smoothed out for propriety's sake, and the resulting uproar restored my faith in humanity, for that day. That people should so care about their candy! Snickers's parent company, Mars, understood our attachment and quickly assured us that "the veins remain." The rumor was intended to troll Tucker Carlson, who was outraged when the green M&M traded in her heels for sneakers, apparently caving to the woke mob and no longer turning him on. "Miserable, nonbinary candy is all we deserve," the Fox News chyron read, and I can't stop giggling about it, thinking about all the days I myself have felt like a miserable, nonbinary candy: sweet and sad and ready to crack.

Let's get the Snickers wrapper out of the way: this is a standard, middle-fold crimped wrapper, fine and serviceable, not too tight, not too loose, and the ad campaign with the adjectives in place of the candy name is great, even if I feel a bit pigeonholed and super-targeted by "hangry." Other words have included "befuddled," "snarky," and "cray cray," which, thank God, no one says anymore. The company refers to these as "symptoms" (of hunger), but I imagine them as a lineup of alternative Snow White buddies, peckish influencers jockeying for relevance. The words look surreal, stretching across the wrapper in blue and white, both familiar and not, the candy bragging of its ubiquity: you would know the font meant Snickers no matter what it said or where it appeared, like those brain teasers where all the vowels are removed and you can still read the message. Cognitive anthropologists call this a minimally counterintuitive concept: something that perfectly conforms to all expectations except for one shift, and is thus rendered even more memorable than something totally familiar or completely new.

The only consistent flaw with this candy is: when you go to pull the wrapper open, grasping that seam that sticks out at the end, you nearly always get this little triangle of plastic that rips away, doomed to end up littering the ground by the thousands, and then you have to pull at the wrapper again to really get the thing open. The moment of opening a candy-in-hand—that first rip, pop, or turn—should be the split second when anticipation transmutes into enjoyment, and having to essentially open Snickers twice each time is annoying. But it's also true that the repetition allows desire to grow just that tiny bit more before it's fulfilled.

Okay, but now we've got the thing open, and if you're selectively anal-retentive and lackadaisically environmentally minded like me (Generation Captain Planet represent), you've slipped that annoying little triangle of trash into the bigger wrapper for safekeeping. I always remove the bar entirely; I don't believe in holding on to carefully folded-back wrappers while I'm eating, lips brushing the plastic, fingers finicky and clean. Just get in there. Those veins on top make the shell just a bit thicker, and the other three sides are a bit heftier than on other candy bars, too. Overall, the chocolate texture here seems just right—a good middle ground between firm and melty, substantial enough to hold the fillings. The base is nougat. Nobody knows what nougat is, but it's a good texture, a classic component you don't even really notice. It's the carrier for the caramel and peanuts on top, and works nicely to cut the caramel goo texture so it doesn't stick in your teeth too much. The peanuts are "fresh roasted," but what does this mean? They're crammed into the bar right after roasting, I suppose? Who knows how fresh any of it is at a gas station in the middle of the Oklahoma prairie, but only rarely does the age of a Snickers seem to make much difference. This is in contrast to another excellent caramel-and-chocolate bar, the Twix, which would be a better candy if not for the inherent freshness gamble, because it gets strange when it ages, the cookies going stale, the chocolate flaking off the ingredients. Another vote for nougat, whatever it is.

Snickers is best eaten on the run, snagged at isolated gas stations and eminently un-isolated bodegas. In New York, before I moved out here to the plains, I would frantically skid into my corner bodega on the way to the train, late for a reading or a show, about once a week. The peanuts make it dinner: 215 calories, eleven grams of fat, okay. I didn't know then that I was using candy bars just as they were originally intended: as a "nourishing lunch" for hungry men and rations for exhausted soldiers in World War I, candy breaking the dainty confines of beribboned gift boxes and moving into a more masculine market. In a reversal, women's magazine ads would later suggest slicing candy bars and arranging them on a plate, to conform to midcentury standards of delicate presentation. The introduction of the single-serve, individually wrapped candy bar to the domestic market not only satisfied the returned soldiers' cravings but suited the increased pace of life in postwar America: people began eating and snacking on the go, no longer able to sit down for three meals at home. A Hershey bar was, by the company's own testimony, "more sustaining than meat." There I was a hundred years later, an AFAB person using candy as a meal like a rushed boy soldier: miserable nonbinary candy strikes again.

Caught in the fast-forward flow of history but myopically aware only of my own immediate destination, as most of us are, I'd stretch toward the high counter and ask one of the Yemeni guys who ran the place—were they brothers?—for one Snickers, please, and lay my dollar and two quarters down in a way that I hoped was quick but not rude. How many ways

are there to telegraph *I'm running to the train—please hurry?*
It's the default mode of serving in the city, a near-frictionless
speed you miss terribly when you move away, doomed from
then on to twitch with suppressed impatience at the cash
registers of nearly empty Walgreens stores, doing your best
not to look like an East Coast asshole.

One bodega guy, the smallest, with the mustache, would
always ask me to repeat myself, and it's true I mumble and
it's true his English wasn't the best, both factors preventing
us from ever enjoying friendly banter or getting to know each
other much at all, even as frequently as I came in. The only
reason I knew they were Yemeni was because another one of
them mentioned having been gone from the shop to attend
that protest at JFK airport's Terminal 4 back in early 2017.
Learning this made me even gladder that I'd gone to the protest, that even if we couldn't talk about much, we could be
united in our opposition to this orange asshat.

These guys always took care of me; the one who seemed
to be everybody's father specifically asked me what kind of
ice cream I'd like to see in the cooler (Häagen-Dazs Dulce
de Leche or, in a pinch, Ben & Jerry's Americone Dream)
after seeing me dive into the case three or so visits in a row
to find only coconut and rum raisin. Anyway, this was the one
bodega of the three (three corner bodegas in my immediate
two blocks) where I never saw a customer and the counter
guy argue nastily, so that's another reason I preferred it, even
though it was cramped, the dusty, off-brand ATM carried a
disconcerting air of identity theft, and it was a thousand de-
grees in summer, when they keep the Snickers in the cool
deli case, which is nice, because when the nougat cools it
does this thing where it kind of breaks when you bite it, very

satisfying, and the caramel hardens up, and that makes for a longer meal; you can take these tiny bites and melt them in your mouth, one by one, and if you don't get self-conscious about sitting there having so much pleasure on the train, you can make the thing last nearly to Atlantic-Barclays. Speaking of the deli case, I never got a sandwich there. I always got sandwiches at the bigger bodega. I have no idea why; it was just one of those city patterns you lock in and never have the time to reconsider. In eight years, I never got another candy in there, although they have the usual Milky Way/ 3 Musketeers/Starburst/Reese's spread. I came in about once a week, and each time, I got a Snickers, or ice cream if the father had stocked it for me, or a bubble water, or cash. One time I rolled in drunk and got some Toast Chees. That's it. This place was for Snickers.

So this one guy, whose name I used to know and have forgotten—I haven't lived full time in New York in a few years, although I still have my apartment, sublet to a series of friends, because although I have no exact plan for return, I'm still "based in Brooklyn," I still want to be part of that hectic, no-time-for-dinner energy, however distantly—this one guy never heard me on the first round. So I'd repeat the request, not irritated even though late, a little smile maybe tugging at the corner of my lips, because I couldn't help but find it entertaining. Here I was again, that girl with the short platinum hair, sweaty and late, asking for the same thing she always did. I was utterly predictable, if a bit of a mumbler. I'd repeat myself, and he'd reach down into the case and pull out my Snickers, and I'd pay and be on my way.

But one day, in the middle of those years, I saw him just around the corner, just walking somewhere, maybe leaving work, none of my business really. I smiled and tilted my head, the universal acknowledgment that passes between daily acquaintances seen slightly out of context (a minimally counterintuitive moment). His face stayed serious, as it always was, the seriousness of a pensive boy, no male hardness to it at all. Something between shyness and worry. Then, just as we were passing each other, right into my ear, after our faces could no longer see each other, he said under his breath, "I love you." I took two more steps, slow and long, sort of floating on surprise and doubt. Then I stopped and turned. He was fast, a brownstone or two away already, and what was I going to say? "Did you just say 'I love you'?" I was crazy to have heard it. But what else did I hear? What else sounds like "I love you"?

The next time I went in for a Snickers, he asked me, once again, to repeat myself. I don't know what it would have taken for us to really understand each other. Maybe he was just trying to prolong the exchange. Or maybe he knew that I would enjoy it more if I had to ask him twice.

On Milk Duds

Pliant and gooey at room temperature, rock hard when cold. In the car on a hot day, forget it. Not even I would try to save that molten mess; do your penance by throwing them out. Stick to Tootsie Pops if you can't manage your supply.

Rarely have I had Milk Duds outside of a movie theater. They're a good pick because a box can reasonably last you two hours, as you must melt down each one in your mouth a bit before chewing. You can really savor them, passively letting your saliva remove the chocolate coating first. The chocolate itself is fine, a little liquid sugary rush before the main event, the caramel inside, the milky dud itself. Press hard with your tongue and you can flatten the lumpy nugget against the cathedral of your mouth, giving you greater surface area and contact with more taste buds at once. Massage that layer with your tongue until it disappears, or skip the flattening and pick a moment to move it all over onto your molars and chew. Somehow, despite nearly four decades of devoted sugar consumption, I don't have any fillings (at the time of this writing), so I can chew right into them early if I want, enjoying how they take the imprint of my teeth, oozing over onto the gums on either side, salivary glands spraying like a lawn sprinkler.

If you're really paying attention when you first put the dud on your tongue, you'll detect a little moment that feels like a thin skin slipping off, before you even taste the chocolate. This is confectioners' glaze, a clear coating that gives Milk Duds and many other candies (candy corn, Whoppers, Jelly Belly beans) their shine, keeping them from getting welded together in the box while preserving their shelf life. It's otherwise known as shellac—derived from the excretions of a

beetle, usually *Kerria lacca,* which lives on trees in Southeast Asia. It's thus *also* known as beetle juice, which as far as I can tell has little to do with Michael Keaton's best and most obnoxious role. To make shellac, the branches onto which the bugs excrete their resin (don't google this; really, don't) are harvested and crushed, which of course results in many bug deaths (100,000 per pound, plus the trees). The material is processed and purified, so you're not *really* eating bugs, but still, no Milk Duds for vegans. And, yes, this is the same shellac you see shining from your grandmother's nice coffee table. Most shellac is harvested in India, where a large percentage of the population, being vegetarian, can't eat any candy made with it. Europeans likely first encountered shellac when the Portuguese colonist Vasco da Gama landed in India in 1498, proving once again that there is no subject, even one as joyous as candy, that you can research for a day or so without bumping into violent conquest. Attention can deepen an experience, and also ruin it.

The thing about Milk Duds at the movies is that they cannot be eaten mindlessly, like popcorn or Junior Mints. Even if you're not distracted by issues of commerce and colonialism, the focus it takes to handle them will split your attention—if you try to eat them while watching a Christopher Nolan movie, you will have no idea what is going on. I usually prefer my pleasures one at a time, so I can give each singular focus, get as much enjoyment out of each second as possible, so watching a movie while eating candy causes an ever-so-slight static in my channels. Candy, then, served for me as childhood mindfulness training. Sometimes I don't get candy at the movies at all, especially if I really want to focus on the film. (See also: my opposition to the whole Netflix-and-chill hookup paradigm.

You can touch me afterward, but by then I'll be too sleepy.) But a maximalist gesture itself can bring pleasure—giving yourself permission to experience more than one exciting thing at a time, the self both agent and beneficiary of generosity—so the pleasure of Milk Duds begins at the moment of ordering, the moment of choosing indulgence over focus.

On Chunky Bar

This one gets points for shape, even though the shape makes it harder to eat. It truly is chunky: a square divided into four sections, with tapered sides, like the base of a pyramid. Kind of beautiful, really, with very deep channels between the sections to encourage you to break it up ("to share," they say, but I never wanted to, have always been glad I didn't have siblings). There's one ridge around the wide-angle foot and one carved around the top. Candy as crown molding.

I would usually break mine in half at least once, although the break was never clean; there was always a peanut or a raisin sticking out of one side, a hole left behind on the other, sometimes tiny crumbs of peanut spilling out. I would lick my finger and press it to the table, starting with these scraps. If a half peanut stuck out of the break, I would trim it flush with a nibble before taking a real bite. The Chunky bar was otherwise very close to my ideal of fastidious enjoyment, composed of one clean right angle after another. Only a candy as hopelessly messy as Butterfinger could disrupt my ritual performances, but that sort of release was years away.

At some point in my childhood, going to the movies meant the agonizing decision between Raisinets and the Brach's box of chocolate-covered peanuts, but the Chunky freed me from this dilemma, holding both raisins and peanuts in its classical pediment. In that way, it felt a little like cheating. The chocolate was especially hard and glossy, the shape difficult to get your mouth around. You'd gnaw the sloped edges, working your way in, feeling the strength of your teeth. It was a lot of work, the sort of thing you only want to eat at home, without witnesses. I seem to remember that we kept them in the freezer, but that can't be right. We didn't do that with any other chocolate; why would we do it with this one, already so solid? It must be a conflation memory with the Klondike bar, also square.

I ate one of these at my friend Megan's house when we were very young, I'm sure of it. She lived in a dark place and her dad was Tim, a skinny blond guy who always reminded me of Tom Petty. (I was the sort of six-year-old who knew all about Tom Petty.) I even got it into my head that Tim (was his name really Tim? There were two other Tims in our life, it can't be . . .) could play guitar, although I never saw him do it. He probably had long hair, at least. The house had low ceilings and that fake wood paneling with the rough black paint dividing the sections, held up with shiny silver tacks. Megan and I always played with My Little Ponies, which lightened the scene enough to be fun, despite the fact that the place

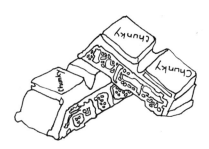

felt unsafe somehow. Illegal things were happening, or we were forbidden from the living room, or maybe Mom always seemed nervous when we arrived, or maybe I just felt strange because their house was cluttered and a bit unclean. (Yes, it was Tim. All the Tims had homes like this, places that were fun for adults and vaguely scary for kids.) But My Little Ponies were always simple sparkly fantasy for me—horses plus magic, what could be better?—back when they were pure, more horselike, before Bronies and before the new generation of the toys, which look like sexy K-pop stars. I think of us playing My Little Ponies, taking breaks to gnaw on some chocolate, and I see us in a bright spot vignetted by darkness I didn't then understand, a shadow that seemed like it would take over when I left. I barely remember eating the Chunky at Megan's house, and I didn't know anything, really, about her life. I still don't. I just seem to remember wanting to share something nice with her before I left.

On Twix

A fresh Twix is pretty much perfect. Like Rolos floating on cookie pontoons, with both crumbly and chewy components and a good slip of chocolate to hold it all together. Their marketing has long celebrated selfishness—two for me,

none for you—but it's disingenuous, because they are too small to share, really, let's be real. I can share Preston with other people—there's plenty of love to go around—but you're not getting my second Twix.

Moderation is one thing, austere restriction another. I've been known to overdo it, and although I obviously don't buy into the moral panic about sugar, I don't think my eating habits would make good public health policy. But I am into living while you're alive. Take the whole serving, butter that bread. Eat until full. We're not going to be here that long.

On Dove Milk Chocolate

Dove chocolate was created in 1939, but when I eat it, I always think about its 1990s ad campaign, which relentlessly emphasized luxury and sophistication. The most memorable ad shows a beautiful woman clad in rich brown silk walking slowly through a room draped in more rich brown silk as delicate piano notes play. As she reclines, her skirt fills the screen, rippling as it transforms into "pure *silk* chocolate." (The special effects still look great, and delicious.) Somehow this whole scene would be wrapped and waiting for you at the grocery store checkout. Without explicitly saying so, Dove

announced itself as the refined alternative to Hershey's, that waxy brick produced in Olde Colonial Pennsylvania, useful only for s'mores and, even then, so mediocre that you might leave behind a smeared chunk of it on the wrapper as you crawled into your tent, to be thrown away in the morning.

Dove chocolate was ease and sophistication, the Grey Poupon of mass-produced chocolate, a logical extension of the upwardly mobile desires of the 1980s and early 1990s. It was the candy you wanted to eat while watching *Lifestyles of the Rich and Famous,* drinking Sprite out of a wineglass with your mom. Dove rode the wave of products made more desirable via a French or British or otherwise vaguely European air—sitcom breaks providing glimpses of a rarefied world. The I Can't Believe It's Not Butter couple reunited in an opulent train station, their love sealed with an on-platform exchange of a cholesterol-free muffin. The fluffy white Fancy Feast cat, steaming off to unknown locales on an ocean liner, tiptoed up to his little crystal bowl and took delicate bites with his flat Persian face.

The epitome of this marketing vibe was the Viennetta ice cream cake, a whipped-up version of ice cream between crunchy ganache layers, like a dessert lasagna or a coffee-free version of tiramisu, that billed itself as the peak of sophistication "for the whole family." It was meant to be Vienna in ice cream form, made even more exotic by additional consonants. Even as a kid, though, Viennetta left me cold—the flavors were weak, the ice cream strangely fluffy, the crunchy chocolate too breakable and cheap, the thing itself, it turned out, a far less sensuous experience than watching the commercials. Aspirational luxuries were no fun when revealed as such; they only made you feel poorer, duped.

Dove chocolate was billed as "silky smooth," and as I watched the ads for a candy that had not yet reached us in Maine, I anticipated this smoothness warily, having been let down by the pronouncements of various treats trying to punch above their weight. Flowing ribbons of chocolate were the standard for candy ads (as George Costanza would later exclaim, "They all have swirling chocolate in the commercial!"), and I knew the implied smoothness rarely materialized. Living in rural Maine, we often had to wait to experience what we saw on TV, and if the fancy thing was truly expensive, Mom would never buy it. But the Dove chocolate bar appeared one day at the grocery store checkout, and the price was fine, maybe slightly more than Hershey's but nothing to bat an eye at, and we bought one, and as I bit into it in the car on the way home, the chocolate really was silky. There was no better word.

Dove chocolate comes in perfectly sized little domed sections. Bite one off and it melts on your tongue immediately, gone so quickly that it's no wonder the bar has become bigger over time. It has the Reese's Peanut Butter Cup problem—it disappears instantaneously. And so Dove's next innovation was a bag of individually wrapped nuggets called Promises, tucked into foil with inspirational quotes printed on the inside, the sugar and silkiness as well as the spiritual encouragement compelling you to open and eat one, and then another, and then another, and then just one more. In this turn to folksiness, you had a sense that this was a warm company, and research shows that it was family-owned from its founding, in 1939, when it was started by a Greek immigrant in Chicago named Leo, to 1986, when Mars absorbed it, as it has absorbed so many other small candy concerns. Who knows what the small-batch Dove tasted like, but Mars did it right, and Leo's son, Mike, who took over a few years before the sale to Mars, no doubt was comfortable for the rest of his life, reaching a pinnacle of wealth that Leo might have dreamed of while slinging ice cream and candy on a windy Chicago street corner.

Having reached greater financial comfort myself, I now feed Fancy Feast to my Ziggy, and sometimes when I pull open those delicate golden cans, I think of how hard Mom worked. I've tried to buy him healthier, more expensive food, but his little street-cat stomach rejects it. I know just how he feels.

On Toblerone

Toblerone always make me think of airports, motion, wistful departures. My mother flew only once or twice in her thirty-year life. I was with her the one time I'm sure about—we went to Florida, for our only out-of-state family vacation. (New Hampshire doesn't count.) It was me, her, and Dale. I don't remember him on the plane, but I remember her. She gave me the window seat, and was just as charmed by the clouds as I was. They were opaque white, voluminous and heavenly.

I was about eight and she was thin and we easily shared the space as she leaned over me in wonder. We had a little 110-millimeter film camera for the trip, but we didn't think to take a picture out the plane window—this was before everybody photographed everything. We just watched the clouds in motion, and felt our motion above them, without the need to freeze-frame a single image. We let memory do its work.

A couple of years before, we'd lived in a terribly ugly house (we called it the Dump) and Mom and Dale had repapered my bedroom walls with towering pink clouds, accented with little V's of seagulls flying into the distance. We all worked on it together. I was tasked with matching up the pattern. It was one of the most loving things they did for me, and now, in this plane, that pattern was coming to life, and in 3D. It had never occurred to me that clouds had tops, and that those tops could look so solid, so real, as though Mom and I could step right out onto them, fall softly backward and lounge fully supported, walking out of the life where she had to go to the factory every day and into one where I could do nothing but read, if I chose, and she could stretch out on our cloudy lawn forever, sunbathing and listening to the radio. It was a lovely daydream, like the ones I had in my pink room, the ones where we had all the money in the world and flew wherever we wanted.

The next time I flew, I did so alone. One aunt put me on a plane and sent me to another, Maine to Texas. Maine was fear and loss and dark, wet woods, and Texas was sunlight and a burning blue sky that came all the way down to the ground. Clouds only on tornado days.

My next flight of any consequence was in high school: a trip to France and Spain, a privately organized venture including about twenty kids from my school and another nearby. My friend Jen's mom was involved, is probably the one responsible for my having known about it at all. The money came from the few thousand dollars I'd inherited from Mom's profit sharing at the Shoe Shop. It was the first major thing I did with it, before I bought a car so I could leave behind family, who would breathe a sigh of relief when I did. The rest went toward college.

Sixteen-year-olds can grasp only so much about a foreign place, especially when they're suffocatingly supervised, but I had a moment alone at the Louvre in which I cried in front of the Winged Victory of Samothrace, standing on a marble landing while people flowed around me. I wasn't even distracted by feeling like a cliché, and for once I was free of that old suspicion that I wasn't so much feeling as performing a feeling. This pure moment of ecstatic reaction made the whole trip worth it. (Stendhal would have been proud.) The rest was bonus: I tipped a cute French waiter about five francs for bringing me a slice of chocolate cake, I eye-flirted with another boy while touring the gardens of Versailles, I climbed the five hundred steps of the Sagrada Familia, I shaded my eyes from the light flashing off the Gaudí mosaics in Barcelona. I stayed up too late with my roommates, laughing about nothing, and our fatigue made the days hazy and dreamlike. And I ate crème brûlée and crema catalana every chance I got, always carefully cracking the top first.

And, of course, there was Toblerone. Toblerone in the airport, Toblerone in each gift shop, tiny snack-size Toblerone greeting us in hotels, each one stamped with the craggy top of the Matterhorn, a symbol as Swiss as chocolate itself, with a rearing bear hidden in its negative space. I had never seen this candy before. Its shape—a long bar of triangular peaks and valleys, which you either have to break off with your fingers or bite off while they poke the roof of your mouth—made it slightly hard to eat, and I read this as the difficulty that comes with sophistication, connected to other foods that you had to learn the procedure for, like raw oysters (which I didn't dare to try yet) or escargots (which I did, and liked) or artichokes (which I knew only as illustrations on food pyramids). The Toblerone chocolate was silky and wonderful, more evidence that pleasures were finer abroad, as I'd suspected, and the tiny flakes of toffee it held in suspension appeared and re-appeared as surprising sparks of flavor. Toblerone, at its full size, comes in a triangular cardboard box, perforated on one end to make a little hinged door—a great candy for traveling, its geometry protecting it from getting crushed in your bag.

I took home four or so bars of Toblerone; they probably didn't last a week. My haul also included La Vosgienne hard candies, in their beautiful round tins, and Mon Chéri choco-lates, which I didn't realize were filled with brandy until I bit into one at school. A straight-A student, I scandalized myself by imbibing booze in the lunchroom. I wondered if I could get a little buzz if I ate them all, then didn't try it. (A British men's magazine calculated that you'd have to eat twenty-three of them to get drunk—which I could have done easily.) Looking back, I wish I'd cut class to drink beers in the woods, just once or twice; I wish I'd taken some of that small inheritance and backpacked through Europe, taken some risks earlier in life, outside of the structure of school. But back then the odds seemed so against me, against many in my rural public high school, where four towns made up a student body of 220 and we were all compelled to take the ASVAB military aptitude test but had to drive half an hour to another district to take the SAT. I did have the one study-abroad year in Australia, but Mom would hate to know that her departure made it harder for me to explore, made me cling to safety. She would have wanted me to take far more flights, as she never could. But still, there were temptations and pleasures to call me, and they did call me. I always think of her when I'm above the clouds, and I think she would be proud.

On World's Finest Chocolate

An absolute mockery of a moniker—the name should instead be Barely Adequate Chocolate. Mostly known as "fundraising candy," these are the narrow bars that kids sell to raise money for their soccer team, choir, or, in my case, junior high marching band. Later in life, I would see families selling these on the subway in New York, fundraising for their lives, it seemed, and feel a pang of complicated nostalgia.

I joined the band under duress, amid the disorientation of my recent move to Texas to live with my army aunt, Tootsie, after my mother's death, compelled by Angela, my very thin, feminine next-door neighbor, who wore crisp pastel polo shirts and little skirts and silver necklaces with delicate charms. Despite my big flannels and ripped jeans, she liked me, but she also simply hated doing anything alone. Right before classes started that fall, we had a consultation with the bandleader, Mrs. Costello. We got dropped off at the band hall—an outbuilding covered in beige metal siding that gave off visible waves of heat, like many of our classrooms in that rapidly expanding district—and took our turns standing in her office.

She was a formidable woman—although short, she radiated taut energy, from her quick feet to her indomitable hair, permed and blown out and teased and highlighted and hairsprayed, a tortuous, epic lion's mane. She was a small-town Stevie Nicks. She wore dark blue eyeliner, precise and all the way around, like my mother had, and she was warm, really, despite her iron-handed drive toward perfection. All this I would soon learn.

That day, I encountered a steady presence with an encouraging smile. She asked me what instrument I wanted to play, and in a rare fit of girlishness I said flute, but when she handed me one, my lips could not even begin to make the embouchure, and all the other twelve-year-old girls must have come in and begged her for flute, so I was assigned clarinet, which ended up suiting me just fine. Middle range in the band, sometimes melody, sometimes harmony, high notes a treble thrill in the fingers, low notes a pleasing rumble in the chest, the instrument itself nicely a little hefty but nothing big enough to stand out. Angela got flute, of course, and would later graduate to piccolo, a great honor that I hope at least partly compensated for her inability to make the top rung in the cheer squad.

Never previously a joiner, I took to marching band with the enthusiasm of a convert. It was a stellar band, 250 kids split into three groups by talent, connected to a dominant football team in a public school district full of families with money. I wasn't passionate about practicing, but I was good enough to average second-to-last chair in the top group. This meant that I was sucky in the best group, and sometimes I wished I was a little worse, so I could be excellent in the mediocre group, but it's just not in my nature. In state band competition, we would earn top scores, flooding the field with elaborate formations, moving with high-kneed steps and diagonal crossovers, the judges in the box up high evaluating the precision of our movements via the pristine white tops of our hats and the blinding white of our shoes. In the height of the season, we practiced both during school and before it, showing up at 6:30 a.m. in the raw desert cold to drill "God Bless America" or "Lonely Goatherd" over and over and over. Downtime on the buses or in the band hall was silly, full of gossip and crushes and pranks. It felt good to submit my will to something larger, to be shown the steps and do them, to feel the feedback of my own breath creating vibration and sound. My mother's death was right at my back, mere months earlier, and I constantly felt like I was flying apart, or else held under a volume of immobilizing water. I drove myself academically, constantly studying and writing papers, correctly seeing school performance as my best chance to pull myself up. Only in band could I relax my own relentless push, only in band did I know just what to do and blithely do it, competently enough but without obsession. I wasn't naturally talented, I got terribly nervous for chair playoffs (solos in front of the whole group, to determine rank, where I learned that cold feet was a literal thing that could happen to your body), and I never practiced as much as I meant to, but I was part of something, I had a part to play, and the music paused the relentless voice in my head that said life was pointless and I should end mine.

The other thing that voice told me, and had long told me, had been telling me since I was seven years old, was that I was too fat, and that being fat made me worthless. I had occasionally been a "chubby" kid, and in addition to suffering my grandmother's judgment, I had been mercilessly teased by my classmates. But by eighth grade I was thin—too thin. I can see it in a photo my aunt took of me and Angela, wearing long purple dresses, our hair curled and pinned up, heading out to a dance. The bone of my shoulder makes a steep, angular cliff of my upper arm, and there's a hollow depression at my temple. At the same time, when I transport my consciousness into that moment, look out from my own eyes, I feel once more gigantic and ungainly next to Angela, who was three inches shorter than me, naturally birdlike and delicate. She hadn't yet hit puberty—I was a young woman and she was a girl, but that didn't matter to me. I measured my body against hers, and against several pairs of my mother's jeans. I got smaller and smaller, and no one said a thing.

At home with Tootsie, in the tense atmosphere she created, where an inadvertent wrong move could earn you a precisely cutting comment that made you feel like the most foolish fool on the planet, we ate dinners together but usually fended for ourselves for breakfast and lunch. I picked at the dinners, spent the rest of the time in my room. For breakfast I scooped cornflakes into a bowl with a measuring cup. For lunch I snuck out like a rodent, tense and watchful, to microwave a single corn dog or build a slender turkey sandwich. Whatever I ate was always too much, by my own estimation. I didn't really know about salads and wouldn't have eaten them; I had a kid's palate, and still do. Of course, if there was candy in the house, it was immensely difficult for me to leave some for my three- and five-year-old boy cousins.

Angela and I regularly weighed ourselves in the bathroom she shared with her little sister, scribbling down our numbers to track our progress. Then we would pore through her collection of glossy fashion magazines, searching for the weights of thin, beautiful actresses and wondering aloud how someone could possibly be *x* pounds (the numbers were low, low enough that I won't repeat them here) and tolerate herself. We were technically smaller than these women; why didn't we feel hot yet? I remember these numbers because we were so fixated on them. I'm almost glad I retain them, because now I can see just how punishing and warped our attitudes about our bodies—all female bodies—really were.

Band was our best diversion from our rituals of feminine grooming and restriction. The group was incredibly well provisioned, but student activities always need more money than a school will allot, and isn't it important to cultivate an entrepreneurial spirit in children? And so came World's Finest Chocolate. We were each given a case of the stuff to sell door-to-door or however else we could, and let loose upon the city of San Angelo. Angela and I went around our neighborhood together, moving toward the bigger houses, following the money toward the golf course. For the first time, I saw circular driveways made with mosaicked pavers and chandeliers in entryways and landscaping where the grass stood as neat and trim as a carpet, flowers professionally healthy. People came to the door, in the middle of a Sunday afternoon, in nice clothes, never pajamas or sweats, the fathers' beige pants carrying a knife-edge pleat down each leg, the mothers in cardigans with pearly buttons. I wore my nicest T-shirts and tried not to sweat or gawk. Angela and I split the take.

After a few weekends of diligent doorbelling, I still had half a case of chocolate left, despite the fact that I was regularly eating them. This felt like theft, even though I knew I'd be responsible for paying for them, so really it was purchase (which meant that in the end my numbers were better than Angela's, it's true). We band kids were twelve to fifteen, and we'd essentially been sent home with drugs, told not to ingest them, and prohibited from raising our prices to cover our snacking overhead. Now it's obvious to me that kids eating them was part of the scam. There the chocolates sat, on my white pressboard computer desk next to my beige Apple IIe—an older model my aunt gave me, something I never would have imagined owning in my mother's house—each the perfect size for a little shot of chocolate. The caramel ones were the most irresistible, mild milk chocolate around a runny golden core, contained in angular domes—like a mini Caramello. They went quickly, and one didn't suffice, sometimes not even two. I'd eat them until I felt sick, watching MTV behind my shut bedroom door, then strip down to my underwear and scrutinize myself in the full-length mirror tacked to my wall, slapping my soft thighs and trying to flex my weak stomach and wishing I could line my eyes heavy and dark like Shirley Manson. The one time I got up the courage, Tootsie, who probably had never worn even a mild sweep of mascara, mocked me. Shamed and discouraged from accessing an edgy, punk aesthetic, I was stuck with the corseted strictures of mainstream femininity—a shape into which I would never fit. Tootsie had never fit this mold, either, but neither of us could see this similarity at the time.

I hated what I saw in that mirror, an out-of-control body that couldn't resist its urges, but no amount of self-loathing could quell my desire for those chocolates, so plentiful, so close at hand. Now I'm saddened that I could ever have been so judgmental of a recently orphaned young teen. That after all she'd been through, I placed so much importance on her being sexy. But that's only part of what I wanted. The truth is, I wanted her to disappear. Marching band, with its strict, coordinated formations, its boxy, shapeless green uniforms, its identical nursing shoes, provided a safe way for her to do just that.

On Malted Milk Eggs

There are Whoppers people, who seek out malted milk balls—Mom was one, bless her—and then there are the rest of us, who grudgingly eat some form of malted milk candy once a year or so, if there's nothing else around. I've eaten plenty of them—usually in the form of pastel eggs, the late April dregs of the Easter candy. They had a soft speckled coating, something like a more sugary version of the yogurt coating on pretzels (which doesn't really have much to do with yogurt).

If we had these around I always wished that instead we had the tiny chocolate eggs, the ones neatly wrapped in brightly colored foil—hot pink, teal, blue, yellow, shining out from the plastic grass in the basket.

The malted milk Easter eggs, though, did have a certain metaphorical purity. While the chocolate eggs were wrapped, the malted milk ones were naked, like eggs. You could pull them right from the grass and eat them—no waste, no hesitation. They were exactly as natural as the plastic grass, the miraculous Cadbury Bunny, the whole manufactured facsimile of spring that was Easter. In Maine, a state that had no real spring, just a few weeks of sliding mud and hatched mosquitoes before the humidity of summer, I didn't perceive a gap between real spring and this illusion. Spring was more a cultural phenomenon than an environmental occurrence. My first college spring in North Carolina was a revelation—weeks of tender, fresh green leaves, flowers of every description scenting the air, a riot of happy flittering birds, baby bunnies hopping through brilliant grass. I'd thought Disney had made all that up.

The malted milk eggs themselves had a nice crunch, disintegrating into exploded dust in your mouth, grinding against your teeth and filling your head with noise. You had to attack them; if you tried to eat them slowly, they'd break into shards and cut your mouth. As the dust hit the wet of your tongue, the flavor was activated. It was something like astronaut ice cream, milky without the flow of milk or the slide of cream, an essence, a concentrate, with, it must be said, an unpleasant tang, likely from the wheat-and-barley component of malted milk. Originally a nutritional supplement for babies, who didn't have the words to complain about the taste, malted milk first became popular in the 1950s, when it was made palatable by the addition of ice cream, which is delicious enough to carry almost any flavor.

But malted milk eggs added up somehow, becoming better as the gluey coating built up inside your cheeks. Still, the whole time, I wanted them to be chocolate instead. It was a pleasure reduced by its not being another. When I see them now, I eat them, enjoying them in Mom's absence. Maybe one day I'll wake up loving them, and then she'll have given me one more thing to love.

On Lindor Chocolate Balls

Sometime in my teens, my aunt Glenice started buying me a pound bag of these each Christmas. It was a perfectly extravagant sort of gift, in a time before I'd eaten very much fine chocolate. The bag was all mine, and when I tried to share it with my aunt Carol, with whom I lived at the time in Maine, she wasn't very interested. Straight-up candy didn't do a lot for her, despite her sweet tooth; she was more of a cakes-and-ice-cream person. Or maybe she just wanted me to have them all. Hers was a muted, pragmatic sort of love, sometimes difficult to detect.

Lindor chocolate balls, or truffles, I guess they're called, are so excellent they're almost difficult for me to talk about, in the same way that something very beautiful is difficult to describe. In both cases, the challenge is in putting language to an intimate experience. But I'll do my best. They're perfectly round, and about the size of a golf ball. Outside is a layer of chocolate just hard enough to encase the sphere of cream within but soft enough to quickly melt if you hold it in your fingers. Each ball has a perfect nipple capping that dome of outer chocolate, which forms a roof over the lake of creamy filling within. I like to bite this little nipple roof off first and peek at the filling, confirming that even in an industrially engineered, perfectly smooth, perfectly spherical candy, there's still evidence, below the surface, of free-form pouring. I love anything that contains traces of its own creation, especially if I'm about to destroy it.

And the pouring is important in the Lindor chocolate ball imagery: their main advertising gesture is a soft-focus television commercial featuring the Lindt "Master Chocolatier," an attractively craggy man in a tall white chef's hat, variously referred to as sexy or sinister by the chocolate devotees of the internet. Most often he is shown dripping chocolate from the swirl of a mixer's tines held at eye level, which is also *our* eye level, as he gazes at that languid flow as though imbuing each truffle with his erotic energy. His face is Old Hollywood handsome, with a strong brow and a significant nose and distinguished lines on either side of a benevolently smirking mouth, and his eyes are hazel, maybe, or green, with a darker,

more solid ring of color around the iris, those penetrating eyes mirroring the structure of the ball of chocolate he's making just for you, the woman on the other side of that eye-level shot. He is not young—he knows what he's doing. He has no lover of his own; he's isolated himself in a kitchen in the remote Swiss Alps so he can devote himself to these chocolates, packets of pleasure that he sends out to all the women of the world. He's a sexual Santa Claus. His internet following is rabid, the articles about him both humorous and breathless, a real advertising coup for a 150-year-old company. They could inform us that their founder essentially invented Swiss chocolate as we know it today when he developed the conching process in 1879, which greatly improved both texture and flavor, but sex sells better than history.

The Lindor ads aren't unique in appealing to sexually unsatisfied women to soothe and fill themselves with chocolate. From the earliest days of commercial candy production, chocolate was positioned as foreplay, with men encouraged to present women with frilly boxes of dainty treats in exchange for unstated favors. A 2012 Pepperidge Farm chocolate cookie ad carries on the sexual snack tradition by promising "waves of pleasure" followed by an "afterglow of chocolate-ness." (Somebody please tell Pepperidge how subtext works.) Chocolate and caramel are forever lustily oozing in TV spots, the apparent sin of delicious snacking a chaste surrogate for sexual adventure. But the appearance of an actual sex object in the form of a man, the man in the form of the tall-dark-and-handsome archetype, is rare. There's something wonderfully outré and explicit about it, just this side of camp. He isn't really hot enough to garner this level of devotion, but finally there's a living, breathing protagonist in the equation.

I agree that chocolate is sexy, and that satisfying any desire of the body is a sensuous act. But I do tire of this *tee-hee* faux naughtiness, wherein the approved outlet for physical urges is a tiny, private act that connects to no one, that can harm no one, the act's frisson predicated on the transgressive thrill of risking weight gain and thus making yourself unworthy of the orgasms you really want.

When I was a teen, the chocolate was only itself—if the hot chef yet graced our TVs, he must have escaped my notice. (I never had a thing for older men.) I knew only the exquisite pleasure of carefully biting off that nipple roof, then placing the chocolate between my teeth and cracking the rest of the shell, then quickly liquefying—oh, it happens so quick—the softer center. I hovered in that suspended moment in which you try to convince yourself that one is enough, before you dive your hungry fist into the rustling bag and pull out some more. To try to be realistic, I'd begin with six at a time, trying to define a serving for the day, or the hour, but I had no control, and the pound bag would last maybe three days, which definitely constitutes a sugar bender, even for me, crazed desire only feeding itself the more I ate.

My forward plunge into the bag was driven, partly, by variety. The pound bags Glenice sent me included milk chocolate, dark chocolate, white chocolate (one of the best white chocolates out there), either peanut butter or caramel, and hazelnut. Hazelnut I can do without—the flavor is unpleasantly rootlike, and the bits of nut interrupt the smoothness. The peanut butter Lindor chocolate ball is nice, kind of an unexpected flavor that I suspect they developed for the American market, but the caramel one is better, in its flavor and its strangeness. It's not caramel so much as caramel-flavored cream, smooth with none of caramel's tensile stretch. The dark chocolate is nice because it's dark but the Swiss version of dark, around 60 percent cocoa, not the 85 or 90 percent or more we see now, especially in organic American chocolate. We've been living through a sort of Dark Chocolate Wars in recent years, a competition to see who can cram the most cocoa in there and still make a bar that holds together, who can perform enjoyment of the bitterest of bitter candies. This is analogous to how some people consume hot sauce, loudly begging for ghost chiles so they can prove, via a completely risk-free activity, how hard they are. Get a Harley already.

I do wish I were immune to the pathetic chocolate-as-sex-replacement equation, but I'm really not—at some point it all got tangled up. (Maybe because I received those Lindor bags in my teens, those years of accelerating lust.) But when do our desires ever align with our intellects? Sex and sugar are connected for me, and if I don't have access to one, I will want more of the other. It's probably no coincidence that the thinnest I've ever been was in the first few months of dating Preston, when we were insatiable, having so much sex I sometimes wasn't sure we could continue dating without ruining our lives. How would we hold on to jobs, maintain connections to family and friends? What roommates would put up with us, how would we ever travel?

In those years when my memoir came out and I could not eat sugar, it was additionally difficult, almost heartbreaking, that, due to the same health condition, I could barely have sex, either. Polyamory was not, then, an endless tour of orgies (although we did manage, occasionally), and even when I was feeling better, my body felt fragile in a way I hadn't previously experienced, which made me more dependent on Preston's kind patience and good humor, his familiarity. I just didn't have the energy to negotiate health issues and boundaries with new people, even if, abstractly, I appreciated that I could.

By 2020 I had more or less healed, but quarantine and lockdown and moving to a small, rather isolated city disrupted the sexual connection between me and Preston for months. He could cuddle, but it was often difficult for him to do more, perhaps because he was wrapped up in the hibernatory impulse that led to fewer babies being conceived at that time. Of course, there were other reasons. We'd had a string of fights, sparked by hurt feelings of the sort that are inevitable when two people are trying to figure out how to love each other. People aim for longevity in love, with the implication that relationships get easier with time. I believe this is true in the long run, but first there's a period when it gets harder—exponentially harder—as a deepening connection reveals each person's terrible old wounds, and that exposure makes us so vulnerable that it's impossible not to hurt each other. We had done our best to repair those hurts, but the work made us cautious. And caution is terrible for the libido.

We were still polyamorous, but of course this was no time to go find anyone else to touch or breathe on, and I burned nightly, longing for communion with this person, this body, just a foot or so away in the bed. I masturbated in other rooms, I read to distract myself, I did a lot of deep breathing and meditating, but still I had a hunger that I needed to fill with something. We got a Costco membership and I discovered the *two*-pound bag of Lindor, and each time one melted down in my mouth, I felt a shadow of the pleasure I really wanted, and I kept reaching for them, as though some as-yet-undefined number of them might add up to satisfaction. I gained weight and blamed the Lindor, and then started subtly turning against myself, thinking that my larger body, and my very voraciousness, had become turnoffs. (Neither of these things was true, I know now.) When I reached for him and got friendly hugs, I shrank in his arms even as my body expanded, and our dry, pecking kisses made me want to grab that luscious caramel cream, imagining my mouth getting wetter as it hit. I observed all this from a space high in my head and could barely stand the sad, late-thirties, self-hating cliché I had become.

I would get up in the night, 3 or 4 a.m., his body warm and blameless beside my own, and I would walk through the dark of the apartment and find myself in the kitchen. I'd pull down the bag and eat a Lindor ball, then another, then another, standing there in the blue light of the stove clock, my frontal lobe still muffled under a blanket, until the comfort lulled me back to sleepiness and I shuffled back to bed, entwining myself around him once more as he slept on.

Eventually I asked him to put the bag up on the highest shelf, one I cannot reach without climbing on a chair, as an additional barrier to midnight fumblings and daytime impulses. I wanted to space out my pleasures more, be awake for them. He became my Lindor chef—if I wanted one, he had to give it to me, and so he once again became able to fulfill my desires. I was reminded that doing so gave him pleasure—I could see it on his face each time—and I finally understood that he had never wanted to withhold anything from me. We began to flirt during the exchange, lengthening it, carefully deciding which of each flavor I would get based on what was left, on what he thought I really wanted at that moment or what I was saving for later. We got to play with power, pretending that he was the only possible agent of my satisfaction, which had never, after all, really been true.

Soon enough the world's new rhythms became familiar, if distressingly so, and our play in the kitchen made its way into the bedroom, and I stopped buying the Lindor, and we both felt less alone.

On Nutrageous

In general, I find myself resistant to innovation in classic candies. Key Lime Pie Kit Kat, Chili Nut M&M's, Espresso Snickers—travesties all. It feels cynical. Like comic book movie sequels and prequels, it takes a beloved childhood experience and spins it into more profit. But at the same time, I love new candy, and I want a world filled with new ones for me to taste or roll my eyes at. I just wish they weren't all coming from the same corporations.

The pace of candy innovation today is nothing compared with the post–World War I candy bar boom, when a printer who produced wrappers estimated, in 1927, that fifteen thousand new types of bars were introduced annually. Many

of these would have been nearly identical recipes, but it also must be true that some uniquely delicious creations were lost not only to time but to the consolidation and corporatization that has resulted in the homogenizing dominance of Mars, Hershey's, Nestlé, and the other giants. I am haunted by those disappeared candies.

But even I can admit that every once in a while, a new candy bar from a mega brand arrives and proves itself worthy. After all, sometimes the sequel is even better than the original—see *Terminator 2, Aliens, Before Sunset*. Nutrageous, for example, is a total winner. It's a Reese's candy, their first new product after Peanut Butter Cups and Pieces. The base material is the peanut butter of the cups, shaped into a long bar, with salty nuts held on top by a layer of caramel, all covered in chocolate. It's a saltier, easier-to-eat version of Peanut Butter Cups, with the brilliant addition of caramel. (Caramel makes everything better.) The name only adds to its appeal. "Nutrageous" recognizes not only its own decadence—two forms of peanut, really?—but its newness and perplexity. It *is* a bit outrageous that a candy brand that had been successfully pleasing a country for seventy years decided to make yet more of itself. Preempting our surprise, and with such a playful word, was a smart move. Nutrageous came out in 1994, the year I lost my mom, when I should have been most resistant to change. Because, really, this resistance is about time, and generational identity—we lock in our candy experiences as children, want our favorites to remain unadulterated. This is the same principle that keeps us listening to the music of our youth, and can make new music unintelligible if we're not careful, if we don't keep up.

On Whatchamacallit

Perhaps Nutrageous, in its naming, took a page from Whatchamacallit, which premiered in 1978, a brand-new Hershey's invention. *What is this thing?* candy eaters thought, and the company replied, *Don't ask us—we hardly know. We didn't even know what to call it.* They let it speak for itself: on the package, against a comic book background of Lichtenstein dots and emphasis vectors, a speech bubble emanating from the candy's name (a word, then, speaking words) announces, "Deliciously crispy!" It recognizes its own absurdity while nonetheless speaking highly of itself and making an argument for its own consumption. Like the Lichtenstein heroines, its speech is self-sacrificial, multilayered. It's the first ironic candy bar.

On Reese's Peanut Butter Cups

Even thinking about these, I feel anticipatory grief. The experience is over before you can really settle into it—one narrow disk gone, then the next. Mulling over my chocolate selection in a gas station, I'm always pulled to these, but have to consider whether I have enough self-control to make them last or if they'll be gone before we've pulled back onto the highway.

Usually I pick something I love less that will last me at least a few exits down the road.

But when I have the patience, when my desire is fine enough that I can spread it out with the requisite deliberation, I get Reese's cups. I can eat them only as a passenger, or sitting alone and still. No multitasking. First I remove the outer wrapper, releasing the sugar–peanut butter smell, setting it aside, balancing the white paper tray on my knees. Then I lift one cup to eye level, or nearly, and peel the thin, black waxed paper off, careful to release it from each scalloped bit of chocolate carefully so the points don't go flying off, never to be eaten. These points are the reason that you often end up with mysterious chocolate smudges on your clothes later, when you swear you didn't drop anything. Once the paper is pulled off, there's often a little messy circle of chocolate coating, with some peanut butter, clinging to the waxy black paper. I press my tongue to it and melt it off. The paper gets folded in quarters and tucked into the plastic wrapper to be discarded.

I might begin by nibbling off those little scalloped edges, all the way around the cup, taking in just the tiniest amount of chocolate. Then I can start in on the neat, round puck, the first bite consisting of the thicker, angled edge, the next bites more peanut butter–focused, with a medium layer of chocolate on the bottom (except for that bald spot lost to the packaging) and a thin coating on top. The peanut butter in Reese's is their own creation. It's a peanut butter cream, really, the sugar aggressive on the tongue, the texture easily giving way and disappearing, never sticking to the mouth or lingering. The cup is gone quickly, but then there's another. Take a breath between the two and linger. There are never enough, unless you've gotten the king size—four in a package—all for yourself. Then you feel self-conscious, the two-puck serving size having been the standard since childhood. But you might feel satisfied by the king size, and why not get enough to feel satisfied? And so Reese's Peanut Butter Cups are, for me, about the battle between giving myself everything I want and settling for what's reasonable, convincing myself that the amount that everyone else has is enough.

On Trader Joe's Peanut Butter Cups

Overrated. Yes, I said it.

People use these to justify their obsession with TJ's, but they're not paying close enough attention. Sure, they come in

a tub, unwrapped, so you can shotgun as many of them as you want. This I support. And they are very smooth inside.

Too smooth.

Quality chocolate, which people mistake these things for, should contain no fats other than cocoa butter or milk. These are boosted with palm kernel oil *and* palm oil, and I've always suspected that this is why they're so smooth, why if I eat one I eat twenty, why they make my stomach feel upset and my whole body feel sluggish and, weirdly, hot. They are a fine mid-level treat, I suppose, but people lose their minds over them. They are cheap for a reason. I'd rather invest in a Justin's peanut butter cup, probably the most expensive candy per ounce that you can reliably find in the impulse area at checkout. For your money you get a much smaller but more delicious treat that won't make your body wonder what just happened to it.

The whole TJ's fandom has never made much sense to me. It's always people who already have money who get most excited about saving it at places like Trader Joe's. Students with rich parents get to save more of their allowances for booze, and upper-middle-class families can reserve some cash to get the next most egregiously overpriced stroller while stocking up for the apocalypse in their gigantic pantries. They do find freakishly friendly people to work there (one of whom is a friend of mine), and the prices are good (although the actual value is sometimes debatable). But it's still a corporation (even more so since the departure of Joe Coulombe—yes, there really was a Joe, a straight-talking yet quirky guy who did, in fact, wear sneakers and colorful T-shirts in meetings with investors). As with Starbucks or In-N-Out, it seems we almost give more credit to corporations, which we expect to be rapacious and vicious, than to smaller companies, doing what good they can with whatever resources they've got. *Ohh, they could have been so bad, but look! They're funding people's college tuition, or providing them with health insurance so they don't die of appendicitis or diabetes or debt-induced hopelessness.* (Just ignore that pesky union busting.) They could have been so heinous, but they are in fact halfway decent, like those peanut butter cups. I'd rather buy something actually good from a smaller company—even though that may be a reductive impulse, smaller not necessarily meaning more humane—or just give in to my lust for the real thing, which is, let's admit it, Reese's Peanut Butter Cups, produced by one of the biggest corporations in the world. At least it tastes more honest.

On Whole Foods Mini Peanut Butter Cups

These come in a plastic tub, with no wrappers, bless them. Once you pry off the top, there's no friction between you and enjoyment. They're a slightly awkward size, a bit too big to pop into the mouth. You have to hold them gingerly and take a tiny bite to get started. But the texture of the chocolate is good, yielding and not brittle or sheetlike, so they bite well. The chocolate shell is thick, good for biting and chewing or for slowly melting, and the peanut butter is smooth but not too smooth. It feels real. These aren't faking anything. They are showing up exactly as themselves.

I last bought these just before Christmas. I rarely go to Whole Foods on purpose, letting myself run in only when I happen to be nearby and need some small thing, a quick errand that inevitably turns into an hourlong extravaganza of

treats and luxuries that I definitely can't afford. Being near all those pristine orchids hypnotizes me into thinking I have money.

This time what put me into splurge territory was a couple of random kitchen tools (I was making soup and needed a strainer, and of course the only one available cost $20), plus presents for Preston's girlfriend Anna. They've been dating for a couple of years, and she and I have a good friendship—easy and respectful, a model for kitchen table polyamory, wherein the goal is to craft your life so that everyone you're dating could at least sit down for a meal together. (We've done that and, well, more.) She has wonderful crinkly blond hair and a slightly husky voice, grew up on a farm in Oklahoma, and was a beekeeper until she became allergic to the little guys. The summer before, we'd planned a party together for Preston's birthday, surprising and embarrassing him with a life-size cutout of him that we set up in a corner with balloons and a background of purple tinsel so everyone could take silly pictures. (We joked that if we really could duplicate him, everything would be easier.) We even had props, like at a wedding reception, and Anna, a part-time photographer, set us up with professional lighting and a real camera on a tripod. He was slightly humiliated and extremely pleased, as he is when we affectionately gang up on him to point out his weird habits and to give him tips on how he can grow as a partner.

We're not the same, Anna and I—she has a wackier sense of humor, is more determinedly self-sufficient. She works as a therapist and as a stripper—two jobs that use her ability to understand what a person needs and to give it to them without giving herself away. (I, on the other hand, am awful at holding anything back, a tendency that can lead to complications, entanglements, and memoirs.) A monogamous relationship can be an echo chamber—you can send reports to friends on the outside, but they can never know exactly what's going on in there. There is no way they can validate your struggles and vexations like a friend who is, in fact, dating your partner and experiencing the same things. Preston is of course a super lucky dude, but between Anna and me (and, previously, Sophie and me), he gets a hell of a lot of feedback.

But Covid broke up the family for Christmas: Preston had tested positive, and if Anna stayed away she might dodge it, but the exposure window was such that she couldn't risk going home to her family-family, either, so she was stuck alone in her apartment through New Year's. So much of love comes down to timing, especially in polyamory.

Anna usually processes sadness and disappointment quickly, but she'd been feeling understandably distraught about her holiday isolation, so I thought I'd get her some things and leave them in front of her apartment door. I figured some tangible evidence that she was included in our holiday would help ease the sting. I got a small, pink bottle of Crémant de Loire, paired with bubbles for her bath, plus those luscious peanut butter cups and fuzzy slipper socks, wrapped in a bright blue bag with a card. It was unfair that I got to stay with Preston and she was alone. My friends often picture the "other women" scrambling for my approval, but I also do whatever I can to try to counterbalance the power I hold from being the cohabiting partner. As with all privilege, it's best to acknowledge rather than deny it.

Living together has been important for me; in times when we've had to live apart, have had jobs far away from each other, I've needed to know the separation is only for a matter of months. I've eaten many a peanut butter cup and every other conceivable candy to soothe my lonely body. Sure, I can have sex with someone else, even sleep beside them, whenever I want, but the someone elses aren't home. I need my home in my home, at least most of the time—the warm smell where his neck curves into his shoulder, the soft kiss good night. She has that only sometimes, although I don't know if he is home to her. She lives with a partner, too, but I don't presume to know how that affects her bond with Preston. I do know they are in love, and she has treated him well. He once told me that he felt good and cared for every single time they'd been together. That's more than enough to inspire some presents from me.

On Symphony

Introduced by Hershey's in 1989, Symphony was their attempt to level up and attract a "more mature" customer, after testing the bar on "upper-class" residents of Los Angeles. It contains more milk and cocoa butter than the original Hershey bar. I bought a Symphony a while ago from CVS, surprised to see

that outdated beige wrapper with the red print and curious about how it would hold up, like when you rewatch a movie from your childhood. Without yet knowing that the base formula is different, I did detect that it was less crappy than the Hershey's flagship. Why wouldn't Hershey's just improve their milk chocolate? This will forever confound me. Is the original formula cheaper? Why wouldn't Americans want their milk chocolate milky and creamy? And why did it take five years of development to come up with the Symphony, a substandard version of something the Swiss had nailed a century earlier?

Symphony comes in two sizes: 4.25 ounces and a "giant" 6.8. A full-size Snickers is around two ounces, so the standard here is already big, resembling a bar of baking chocolate more than a snack. The giant one feels giant in the way the first ultra-big iPhone did: obscene and embarrassing to hold, until the "fuck it" quotient kicks in. Still, the bar is very thin—you don't bite so much as break it, and it kind of floats around in your mouth as shrapnel. This thing should be thicker and of smaller lateral dimensions. It's not very classy to hold a four-by-six-inch board of chocolate up to your face.

The Symphony commercial features, of course, an orchestra playing a symphony, intercut with your standard pouring-the-chocolate-into-an-invisible-mold sequence. A masterpiece of chocolate, it's called, but it's really just a performance of sophistication. Frasier Crane wouldn't have gone anywhere near it.

On Mozart Piano Bar

Like Dove and Symphony, another upwardly mobile candy, this one with a portrait of no less revered a personage than Amadeus himself, sitting right in the center in bewigged profile: hawkish little beak of a nose, ruby lips, dark sculpted brows that Instagram influencers would die for. The sharp cut of his high, rouged cheekbone is echoed in the bright red jacket collar both turned down and standing up, holding a flurry of white ruff. Suddenly the composer's influence on rock star aesthetics is obvious: he's Prince in purple brocade, Axl Rose wrapped in an elegant scarf, whichever Beatle was most glamorous (John, right?), the fantastical Harry Styles. The background of the wrapper is bright red, too, technicolor, more hot rod than velvet settee. "Mozart" arcs above Mozart's head, riding a curve of golden filigree, and black-and-white keys hold up the words "Piano Bar" in fifth-grade-perfect

cursive. Cut out and isolated as they are, the keys look more like a synthesizer than a Steinway, calling to mind my grand-mother's Casio keyboard, with the preprogrammed samba backbeats and the sound effect settings: water droplets in every tone, cat meows.

This is another mise en abyme bar, carrying a picture of itself, the candy cutting across one side of the piano keys, zooming toward the viewer. It's a rounded log shape, like a smoother Baby Ruth, milk chocolate with a bittersweet, decorative drizzle. Inside we encounter a bright green paste. Green being a rare candy color, particularly in chocolate items, I immediately read the back for the ingredients: pis-tachio marzipan, as well as hazelnut praline, accented with rice crisps. A symphony of textures, if you will. I admire the boldness of a pistachio marzipan—marzipan being made with almonds, this is a nut product flavored with another nut product, and the hazelnut brings in yet another, all with no uncomfortable nut texture. All this nut-on-nut action is hard to pull off, but this sticks the landing. The marzipan is the real deal, thick and resistant, unapologetic. The whole thing is very European—no surprise that it's German, made by a company called Reber Spezialitäten. Whoever these Rebers are, they know what they're doing. The rice crisps don't overwhelm, are pleasingly sprinkled throughout, add-ing just enough texture to keep the eating slow, a series of nibbles.

Anna brought this for me, having seen it at World Market while shopping with Preston for decorations for my birthday party. I got to stay home and nest, lean into the homey feel-ing of mid-December. I never would have experienced this unexpected pleasure without her, just as I wouldn't have had an elaborate birthday party with plentiful snacks and half-ironic twinkle lights and tiny fake Christmas trees scattered throughout our apartment. It took the two of them a day and a half to prepare, and she's the more practical of the two, doubtless kept him on track. It was she who brought me a little something extra from the outing, something sweet and unexpected and strange. Whether she meant to or not, she reminded me that something you never would have imagined wanting can end up being just what you need.

On Costco Chocolate-Covered Almonds

Almonds are such a seemingly guiltless food—the sort of thing that femme dieters might count out, one by one, in a sad, 1980s pantomime of happiness—that I am hesitant to include them here, even covered in chocolate. The term "almond mom" resonates for a reason. But the central question is: Are these truly a candy, or a snack?

There are many sweet items, like Little Debbie Zebra Cakes, that bring intense lust and soul-sweeping nostalgia to the surface, but which are snacks, not candy, and therefore outside of our purview here. See also: Froot Loops, those individual Kool-Aids with the twist-off lobster claw top, limoncello (both liquor and LaCroix), and those premade cookie dough servings in the little tubs that don't even presume that you'll make them into cookies. And speaking of the taxonomy of sweetness, right now I can hear a whisper, coming to me from co-ops and farmers' markets, riding a faintly lavender-and-palo-santo-scented wind: "What about fruit? Mangoes and pineapples and peaches?" And I just want to take this

opportunity to say that "fruit for dessert" is the saddest, most infuriating phrase. It is gaslighting to offer fruit to a person who expected to end her day with actual indulgence and not a piece of the food pyramid. "Fruit for dessert" isn't information; it's an argument. A person who utters this phrase is trying to talk me into a concept, usually with an airy, cheery attitude, as though they are doing me a favor. You don't mean "for"—you mean "instead of." What you're really telling me is that we're not having dessert. I might not even have craved dessert on my own, and now I have to sit glumly through the period of time that would otherwise have cake in it. I'd rather just get up from the table.

At least the phrase can serve as a warning, preventing me from imagining a molten chocolate cake and being presented with, at best, pavlova. Just don't misrepresent. Orange segments with cream poured on top is not dessert, and sugary cereal is not candy. We must resist the forces that would call one thing by the name of another. Some sweet things are snacks, some are candy, some dessert. Some, like fruit, are just groceries.

Costco chocolate-covered almonds, though—let's consider why this counts as a candy. First, how do we understand an almond? Although it took us from the seventies until today to figure it out, we now know that almonds are actually really fatty (yes, "good fat," but still) and that they are depleting water reserves in California and elsewhere, so they aren't the harmless little ovals we'd imagined them to be, all dry and self-contained and without consequence. Second, a Costco chocolate-covered almond is hidden in a jacket of chocolate so thick as to render the almond merely a chocolate conveyance device. It's less a chocolate-covered almond than it is a chocolate glob pregnant with an almond. So definitely a candy, a sweet treat laden with the psychic weight of decadence. They come in a tub, like a milk jug with the top cut off, embarrassingly Americanly plentiful, like everything at Costco, and I suppose they're meant for families with three or more children, or daycare centers. But when I buy these, they're for me alone, as Preston, an otherwise wonderful person, "doesn't really care for sweets." (It bears repeating; I can't get over it.) How *do* we decide whom to love, anyway?

These almonds rattle like a low-toned maraca when you leap up and smack them down from a high shelf (a placement meant to slow your consumption), swatting like a cat and catching the tub as it comes tumbling down. The gold screw top, diameter bigger than your hand, makes a good little plate, the taps of almonds hitting it like the happily anticipated fat first drops of a spring rainstorm. Pluck the first one: chocolate firm, just firm enough to not melt under your fingers (and protected by confectioners' glaze), the almond always fresh, meaty, never brittle. Chocolate as preservative—brilliant. The milk chocolate is at the right level, I'm guessing a solid 33 percent cocoa—standard, reliable, no funny business. The first one goes down with a kick from your salivary glands, your body preparing itself, and then you hardly perceive it, rush on to the next. Five or so in and you can finally linger, letting one melt in your mouth until you have a simple almond, a seemingly healthy little break in the bender.

These almonds were a beginning-of-pandemic discovery, found on our first trip to Costco, in March 2020, when I'd moved from New York City to Tulsa so Preston and I could be together at the end of the world. Three months before, he had started a yearlong writing fellowship I was slated to join in the fall, but then I moved early. In truth, our relationship hadn't been doing so well, but that March weekend New York was seized by a rumor that Trump was going to close all travel into and out of the city—trains, bridges, airports. I had to decide: move now or be apart so long that our rift might become permanent.

Once I moved in, we mainly shopped at Costco, where we could stock up and thus go out into the germosphere less often, so I could buy candy only in huge packages. In many ways, I was trading variety for stability. It was a time to commit.

The packaging is basic, cream-colored background, red Kirkland script, no attempt at fancy, opaque "artisanal" branding, so I did not understand at first how addictive these almonds would be, what a commitment a jar of them really was. I did not know how long those months of isolation would go on, how rare pleasure would become, how much we would have to cultivate appreciation for every little good thing, how narcotic these would be, as I sat reading about ventilator deaths and California fires and New York floods and the fall of Kabul. I underestimated the tension I would feel between my small daily pleasures and the screaming, bleeding, burning terror of the world. I would not have guessed that I would arrive here, breathlessly grateful for any small thing, determined to celebrate whatever I can, wherever I can get it.

Costco chocolate-covered almonds also stepped in when, in those early pandemic days, I made a decision not to drink for a while. It was clear to me that alcohol was about to go sharply in either one direction or the other: I would spend the months or years of disaster either sober or day-drinking my way into a hellish depression. I have a bit of a binge-drinking history, nothing that ever quite rose to the level of a problem, and still occasionally feel what I think of as the Thirst, some impulse, unlocked by the second or third drink, to keep going and going, some insatiable desire that's always lurking, held back by a complicated mix of factors. I'll unexpectedly drink much more than I'd set out to, and the next day I'll blearily reflect: it was the Thirst, this occasional evening visitor that arrives unannounced. In March 2020 I had a suspicion that this spirit was hovering, ready to move in permanently. I held it off by eating candy instead. Those chocolate almonds, in almost infinite supply and satisfyingly addictive, were a perfectly adequate replacement. But still, I wasn't pretending they were an intoxicant.

Part of the problem with me and drinking, other than genetics and, maybe, Irish ancestry, is that I bought into, early on, the dominant American mindset about alcohol, where the substance is treated not as a pleasure but as a tool. In his *Mythologies,* the philosopher and essayist Roland Barthes writes that "in France intoxication is a consequence, never a goal; drinking is felt as the exposure of a pleasure, not as the necessary cause of a sought-after effect." Americans could never. We drink to drink, to get drunk: each action must have an appreciable, measurable effect in the industrialized, assembly-line, time-stamped existence that we (Henry Ford) created, which we see as a natural state of living and the rest of the world experiences as an imposition. Even our hobbies are cast as projects of self-betterment, agglomerations of skills. Pleasure for its own sake has no deliverable, so we need a productive alibi not for the dreams produced by wine but for the wine drinking itself: drunkenness as accomplishment and masculine boast, or the release of job-related tension, the more of which you have the more valued you are for your Puritan work ethic. If pleasure comes as a by-product, fine. Pleasure from drinking (both pleasure of taste and of intoxication) is permissible (unlike the pleasure of, say, pure idleness—even naps are justified by their positive effect on work performance, even leisure must be evidence-based) because there's an implied, perhaps inevitable, penance the morning after. Pleasure without consequence is anathema to American consciousness—we can't bear it. I love the taste of many kinds of alcohol, but I always have an ulterior motive. I drink to get drunk, or I drink to perform socially, or I drink to make sure that I fully relax one evening so I can better focus on my work the next day.

Candy, though, is irrational; its consumption produces nothing. It is no dutiful cause seeking an effect. Candy is about happiness in the moment—this exact moment, each subdivided microsecond of melt, each deliriously destructive chomp. Candy happens in the face, where the social and the animal most strongly intersect. The social face is soft, readable, subtle. The movement and shape of more than twenty muscles determine our identities, differentiate us, convey our trustworthiness or lack thereof (illusory or not), our intelligence, our humanness, while those same muscles pulverize objects we've taken into the body. We give little attention to the brutal working of the human jaw, a lever producing seventy pounds per square inch of force, ten times more in anxious sleep as we grind up the stressors of the day, the headlines and domestic conflicts, purely animal in our unconscious state. I managed to avoid alcohol for the first nine months of the pandemic, my longest period ever without drinking, wading back in when it felt safer to do so, when I knew the Thirst wouldn't come to subsume me. Until then I had candy, a wonderfully elemental comfort, but still, my jaws worked anxiously day and night. I had never ground my teeth before, and now I clench all through my dreams, bracing myself like an animal who feels vulnerable in the dark.

On Cherry Republic
Chocolate-Covered Cherries

For the past few years, Preston's aunt Marijane has been sending these to us each Christmas, in a large gift box with other cherry items: gummies, chocolate-covered bridge mix, nut mix with chocolate-covered cherries strewn throughout. They're Montmorency cherries, tart and dark, grown in many places but especially in Michigan, his home state. Cherry Republic is a small company, eighty employees, based up north—not quite as far north as the wild Upper Peninsula, but getting there. I've seen pictures of the area on Instagram. Sleeping Bear Dunes is nearby, a fantastically beautiful spot where rolling grassy hills dotted with little trees come down to cliffs of soft golden sand, edging a Lake Michigan that glows in shades of blue-green I didn't realize were possible in

inland North America. We'll go up there someday, I'm told, when the timing works out, when we have the bandwidth to attend the annual reunion on Mackinac Island, full of lovely people who do not vote as we do. In the meantime, we've had Aunt Marijane's generosity: the dried cherries tart and super sweet, still wrinkled and juicy, almost a gummy texture, the chocolate thick and smooth, convincingly handmade. When you bite them, the chocolate never shatters off the cherry; it's all nicely welded together, even if you bite one in half, holding the other half in your fingers while you savor.

These have superseded Lindor chocolate balls as my favorite 3 or 4 a.m. somnolent snack. I pad out to the kitchen and then rustle in the cabinet like a sleeping bear, hoping I won't wake up Preston, while knowing I am too asleep to be coordinated and quiet. Cherries naturally contain melatonin, and Montmorencys have the highest concentration of this sleep-inducing compound. Melatonin is called the "chemical expression of darkness," because our brains are supposed to make it when the sun goes down. It's reassuring to think that my body, so disrupted by stress and incandescent lights, will at least sometimes still steer me toward what it needs.

This gift helps draw me into a complex ecosystem. Preston's family is a large, connected clan (Irish Catholic and so midwestern as to seem almost fictional), so much more tightly woven than my own, and I love seeing my name on that shipping label, even if every year Marijane, forgetting that we live in an apartment building, leaves off the apartment number and the manager has to come find us, his face a battleground of annoyance and holiday cheer. Christmas, in non-pandemic years, means a huge gathering on Preston's mother's side: six siblings and their dozens of kids and grandkids. (Among the many generous and fine gifts I've received from his mom: a gleaming bread knife. When Glenice comes to my house with that ciabatta, I will be ready.) Once, we played a game where you try to uncover who in the room is the spy, and, knowing almost no one well, I was at a hilarious disadvantage, buried in a tidal wave of loud cousins. But at least they didn't think I was the spy.

Preston and I always go to Michigan for holidays, not Maine, because the branch of my family that hosts holiday gatherings disinvited me forever years ago, when they discovered that I had a girlfriend. I didn't even launch a coming-out, I just replied honestly when, not having recently heard the name of a boyfriend, they asked me whom I was dating. I was thirty-two years old, but I still cried as I drove away that weekend, trees gloriously ablaze with late fall blurring past my windshield as I took curves I knew so well I could drive them blind. I thought of all the teens still cast out, and I thought of my own teen self, dependent on the goodwill of extended family in the wake of her mom's death, correctly sensing that she risked homelessness if she admitted to her desires. Kinder, saner aunts objected to my expulsion, but the tone was set by two uncles, who decided to remain caricatures of difficult uncles: wedded desperately to oppressive gender norms and outwardly hateful of those not like them.

I've moved far away from my people many times, and have a complicated relationship with the landscape that holds them. Mostly I pretend to myself that it's fine that I don't visit my own lakes, my own low hills covered in pines and snow. But when I get the box of cherry candies, I meditate on the drawings on the gift cards that come in the packaging: forest scenes in a charming, slightly cartooned style, crisp ink outlines filled softly with watercolor. The trees and the style remind me of the hand-drawn chamber of commerce map of my tiny hometown of Bridgton, a place I haven't lived in almost thirty years—the bright blue rivers, the green fields, the aerial perspective combined with the lateral, so that select landmarks and businesses were drawn in clapboard detail over the diagram of two-lane roads, the ski mountain rising above the whole scene. Everything made pleasing and manageable, showing only the sweet parts—the Flower Pot, the Gazebo ice cream shop, the Magic Lantern. No police station, no hospital. This image was made for the tourists, of course, but when I think of Bridgton on my best days, it's what I see. Within that picture, no one fought, no one was in danger, no one was cast out. People laughed together near fireplaces that sent up charmingly curled tendrils of smoke. Deer hid behind little trees, trout cheerfully awaited the hook in those spills of blue. In the evening, the sunsets were gentle, and sleep came softly and easily, lasting all night as the whole picture held us there, where we belonged. The map was an idealized place that we could occasionally enter, on quiet days in good weather.

Marijane passed away this year, and I'm glad I saved our last Cherry Republic card, a snowscape with a little red barn in the foreground and tiny people pulling sleds up a hill while a tiny dog bounces around them. It's stuck to our fridge in a layer of pictures and poems and a spring 2020 note from Sophie that reads "Take care of each other." Aunt Marijane was a woman who loved me even though we met only once, who never would have thought to cast me out. She might have forgotten the apartment number, but she always put my name on the box.

Gold

On Ferrero Rocher

'm not sure there's a more overhyped chocolate—I don't know if I've met anyone, ever, who truly loves eating these.

First of all, let me be clear: I love slick packaging, enjoyment that starts with the presentation. But the frantic, sweaty oversell begins here. Starting from the outside, we have a gold-foil-wrapped ball that sits in a tiny brown-and-gold cupcake liner. There's even a name for this liner; the company's website makes sure we know it's called a *pirottino*. As though we might use this word in conversation. "Oh, Ferrero Rocher? In the charming *pirottino*?"

The golden ball is topped with a sticker informing you that you're eating a Ferrero Rocher, in case you forgot—redundant and ridiculous like the thousands upon thousands of stickers on Red Delicious apples, repeatedly proclaiming their identity as though you couldn't identify them by their butt chin, their lack of flavor. The gold foil is thick and crinkled, not smooth, and so begins a journey of unfortunate textures.

Step one is to pluck the cupcake liner off the wrinkly foil ball. Again: Why is this liner even here? The candy never even

touches it. These are cute on cupcakes because they combine form and function, seem almost accidentally charming in their neat pleating. But this thing is useless. The ball is held down with a little nob of adhesive, a bit like rubber cement, so you're sure to immediately mangle the pleats of the liner thing, a small act of destruction disproportionate to your anticipation. Now you have garbage already, and you haven't even peeked at the chocolate. Hopefully the adhesive hasn't stuck to your fingers, where it's destined to transfer to your mouth. So put this little paper thing, this *pirottino,* aside, turn the golden ball over, and pull open its previously hidden wrapper butthole. More garbage. Now you have a bonbon: rough, with the hearty texture of a meatball. Whatever's inside has been rolled in nuts and then coated in chocolate. The visual effect is more forbidding than enticing, jagged like an asteroid. *Rocher* is, after all, French for "rock." The story is that chocolate patriarch Michele Ferrero modeled the candy on Rocher de Massabielle, the grotto in Lourdes, France, where the Virgin Mary appeared to Saint Bernadette. Even I can see the blasphemy in representing the mother of God as a nut.

But to avoid for a moment that intimidating, rough surface, let's pause to reverse course and think about this thing from the inside out, the way it's presented in the golden-lit, inferior-to-Lindor commercials. There are a lot of steps along the way: Rocher clearly wants us to go on a journey. First we have a full hazelnut. *A full nut!* the commercials nearly gasp. *A hazelnut, my God!* Never mind that it's the blandest of nuts, its flavor so weak it's more of an irritant than a provocation. The whole hazelnut is dipped in a "velvety filling," which appears also to be of hazelnut and, in its resemblance to Nutella, is the only good part of this experience. How is Nutella delicious when hazelnuts are so incredibly lackluster? *Texture* is the answer, and I cannot stress this enough: Ferrero has done everything it can to ruin the texture of this candy.

Next, outside of the velvety filling, we have a weak sphere of wafer cookie. I guess this is primarily a structural component, because it's not even mentioned on the website's "discover" description. It would be innocuous if it wasn't so often stale (how does it get stale while so insulated?), breaking in dissatisfying chunks while infusing the bite with a nose-backdraft of cardboard.

The wafer sphere is covered in more chocolate (or that mysterious velvety filling; it's unclear), and the whole thing is rolled in . . . more hazelnut. The effect is macabre: a hazelnut covered in its own cream filling and rolled in the shattered bones of its comrades. The outer hazelnuts are sharp, like tiny gravel, and scrape the roof of your mouth. It's another inception candy, like those strawberry-foil-wrapped hard candies with the gel center, the difference being that those are good.

The sin of poor texture is exacerbated by poor scale. The whole bonbon is too big to put in your mouth all at once, but if you bite it, the construction falls apart, each component separating and scattering, from tiny nut slivers to puffs of cookie. You make a scoop of your other hand to catch it, in a desperate, undignified gesture, out of step with the candy's high-class pretensions. The hazelnut itself cowers in your palm, naked and pale. The two of you are in this together. You feel a bit bad for it, tongue it from your messy palm. You're game, you're down, you've come this far, but in the end you can't escape how anticlimactic it is. It's a hazelnut. Unless you're a squirrel, it cannot carry the show.

It's easy to laugh at the infamous "Ambassador's Party" commercial from 1993, wherein a central-casting butler glides around a wood-paneled room with a golden pyramid of Rocher, received with poorly dubbed compliments in various bad European accents. But if you look closely, you'll see that the guest who pronounces them "Eccellente" is none other than Wolf Kahler, who played the head Nazi in *Raiders of the Lost Ark*. So let's just say his taste is questionable.

In their exuberant packaging, Ferrero Rocher reveal themselves as designed primarily for exchange; if you were buying these for yourself, you wouldn't need all the flashy accessories, least of all the antiseptic plastic box and gold egg-carton tray in which they are nestled. The candy itself is destined for elaborate presentation, too fragile to survive floating around in a bag. It's true that they are greatly valued by immigrant communities in the United States, appearing on Chinese New Year and Diwali, and as daily hospitality gifts. In Hong Kong they are known as "gold sand." My personal disdain for these little chocolate boulders is insufficient to undermine their importance to cultures not my own—let others drag Andes mints if they feel like it. I get it: we're all seeking belonging, we all want to feel that we're at least occasionally living the good life. Under current conditions, that sensation is most efficiently provided by products crafted by multinational corporations. But let the experience of the product be actually good, otherwise the whole exchange is condescending. I just cannot get myself to believe that others actually think this thing is delicious; to me, that sad little hazelnut at the center is clad in the emperor's new clothes. It's the Viennetta ice cream cake all over again.

Yellow

On Warheads Extreme Sour, Lemon

A militant lemon drop. The logo is a cartoon face with crossed eyes and pursed lips, with a nuclear mushroom cloud sprouting from its head. The face is long, like the figure in Edvard Munch's *The Scream,* like Macaulay Culkin yelling into the mirror in *Home Alone.* When I was growing up, this was the candy of fifth-grade boys who pulled out your scrunchie on the bus, boys who disrupted class by punching each other in the shoulder across the aisle, boys who always found the highest point on the playground and jumped off. I hated those boys. They occasionally got in trouble but never seemed to suffer any real consequences, and the "boys will be boys" attitude that surrounded their misbehavior seemed to ignore that they were dominating the rest of us with their loudness, their displays of physical power.

Warheads hurt, burning your tongue and cheeks with citric and malic acid, and that was the point. Those boys ate them while loudly cheering one another on to make sure everybody was paying attention, in some nascent effort to display

masculinity by suffering self-inflicted pain. Scholar David Savran calls this process "reflexive sadomasochism," in which a male subject acts both as torturer and victim so that he can prove he can suffer "like a man." At the time, I didn't have a sophisticated understanding of what I was seeing. I just found it all exceptionally dumb, as I would later find *Beavis and Butt-Head* and *Jackass* dumb. I had some instinctive sense that their display was doomed, that "taking it *like* a man" was pathetic, the comparison only making it more clear that these boys hadn't yet become the thing they were emulating, that maybe nobody at any age ever reached that brute ideal. Candy was meant to be lighthearted and playful, and their loud efforts to leave those childlike and feminized qualities behind struck me as unnecessary and ridiculous. Also, I just thought they were gross. The candies, I mean.

However, I've recently discovered that the pain these candies inflict can actually be healing. My friend Hannah, who runs mindfulness workshops for creative people, taught me that therapists will sometimes give Warheads to patients who are suffering trauma responses during sessions. The intense sour flavor helps those who are dissociating to come back into their bodies and into the moment. It can also interrupt the physical symptoms of a panic attack, distracting the person from their racing heart or sweating hands and thereby interrupting the feedback loop between mind and body. When she told me this, I thought about how bondage or impact play can work as a form of intuitive therapy. I also thought about myself, post-heartbreak and seeking as much sensation as possible as I ate that Scandinavian candy in Guatemala.

The very day after Hannah and I spoke, I found the most moving four-hundred-word review of lemon Warheads from the parent of a thirteen-year-old boy who struggles with ADHD and emotional regulation, who regularly acts out without meaning to and then finds himself mystified and guilt-ridden and humiliated. The two figured out together that if he eats a Warhead the moment he's feeling out of control, the shock of sour helps him calm down. It worked so well the first time that the parent cried while the boy went instantly from fury to laughter. The review was written so tenderly. It's impossible to tell, but I want the parent to be a dad. I imagine a dad and a son, turning pain and confusion into tenderness.

American masculinity values dominance and pain, a sort of unholy suffering, and the gauntlet begins early in life. Reading that loving product review, I immediately felt guilty for hating Warheads and for hating those boys. I couldn't know, back when we were kids, what they might have been struggling with, and how the prevailing culture could have been making their struggles worse by disregarding their sadness. No doubt they disliked me as well, with all my eager hand raising and ostentatious playground book reading. We were all performing whatever selves we thought would help us grow up and get by. Warheads at least provided a rush of feeling to a gender commonly trained out of feeling much at all. Even the most militant of candies can be used to return us to the body, for consolation.

On Lemon Drops

Like many candies, these must have begun in a digestif tradition, citric acid helping break down a heavy dinner. Their color calls to mind limoncello and brings on dreams of Amalfi, of Capri, Greece even, breezes sweeping across a jewel-blue ocean, sandstone glowing warm with the trapped heat of the day. Café tables and candles in wine bottles and heavy red sauce and wine, then the tiramisu, so light you swear you'll never eat it again back home, and then a tiny curved glass of lemon orchards, a sweet astringent punctuation preparing you to head off into the night.

I'm imagining all this. I've traveled so much less than I thought I would, but it's silly to put that in past tense. I'm not yet old, and I don't have kids. Summers largely free. I can

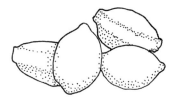

go anywhere. How I wish I had gone, so many places, before smartphones obliterated dislocation.

Lemon drops are nostalgic and technological at once. They're sugar and chemical flavoring, surely divorced from their stomach-soothing roots, but still a ritual and a palate cleanser. Slightly sugar-dusted on the outside, they really light up once you've sucked on them a little. The flavor is gentle, just slightly sharpening the sugar. Your mouth waters to think of them, even though they aren't overly delicious, are merely, let's say, serviceable. You have one and don't need another, or not right away. Lemon will tell you when to stop.

Pink

On Good & Plenty

Lindsay Lohan hot pink with pure white, thick sugar shells that split under your teeth. You can carefully bite down to the black licorice, strip the sugar part off, and suck on the slippery inside, or just crunch through, enjoying the splintery outside and the chewy inside all at once. Good texture play, almost a little too wild for an older candy. The name is excellent: a signal toward satisfaction, an expectation of contentment. They are good, they are plenty; you have plenty and goodness, and the box is enough. Measure out your happiness, capsule by capsule.

On Starburst

Starburst are "unexplainably juicy" and encourage us to "share something juicy"—two wonderfully sexy phrases. It's an accurate flex: they *are* unexplainably juicy. They appear to be a dry little chew, but once you get them going, they squirt into your mouth.

Starburst are just the right size, satisfyingly square. I even like that they are traced with weird trail marks from their journey through whatever huge candy-making machine produces them. The object itself is deceptively utilitarian, corners unfinished, wrapped oh-so-tightly in waxed paper with its own name printed all over, much like the Tootsie Pop toile. Repetition as celebration. Litter as exuberant advertisement. Starburst are better fresh, when they are soft and pliable. When older, they harden but are still nice to gnash. I always squish-test them a little bit in the store, not to decide whether to get them but to see what I'm getting.

The standard Starburst packaging is a long row of them, wrapped up in very thick, foil-backed paper. I'm attracted to candies packaged thusly: Mentos, Rolos, and even Necco

wafers. I like having a satisfying, dense row of something, a bullet cartridge of sweetness to defend myself from the world's disappointments.

In a polarized and fractured world, the superiority of pink over the other Starburst flavors is one undisputed thing. It is, I hope, the only conviction I share with Donald Trump, whose rabid love of these little pink squares has been widely reported. What do I do with the fact that this humanizes someone I otherwise find detestable? That I feel defensive of both of us when *Eater* declares that his "taste in candy is especially juvenile"?

Although I'm bound to feel a small thread of connection to anyone whose candy preferences are so pronounced as to make national news, there were a handful of other times during Trump's presidency when I found him strangely endearing, like a hapless uncle or an overgrown toddler. This feeling was probably displaced love for my literal uncle Carroll, who had the same small, receded eyes, the same strange blond hair—which made me suspect, for a time, that Trump's was natural. Or perhaps, as philosopher Kate Manne argues in her analysis of why the majority of white women voters picked Trump in 2016, I've just been trained to unduly sympathize with oppressive men. I'd see him squinting directly at the sun or mincing down a ramp and I would feel a burst of empathy in direct proportion to my disdain, a brief flash of terrible discomfort. Something to hide, to suppress. I worried that feeling for him, even briefly and privately, meant I was somehow complicit in his hatred and violence. I stepped back and observed myself, a woman taking on the perspective of a gaslighter, an ancient form of self-preservation that endangers those more vulnerable than oneself. But still, he was a person who had been a child and who still craved sweet, bright things. Here, then, was a human, as Mom's killer was also, unfortunately, a human. Could either of them have grown into anyone else? What would have had to change to keep the rest of us safe from the men those boys would become?

And what of those surrounding Trump? Having observed his leader fishing out only the rosy Starburst on Air Force One, House Speaker Kevin McCarthy famously tasked aides with picking out the pinks and reds to make the president a special jar. (It was winter, and the all-pink packages were still a summer-only seasonal release.) I imagine a sad young conservative woman toiling for long hours at her desk, her only respite an ever-growing bowl of oranges and yellows. Girl, get outta there.

The pink Starburst is strawberry, but even though it does contain the actual juice of the fruit, it's really its own flavor, a happy one calling to mind all sorts of innocent images. It is ballerina tutus, girl sleepovers, satin ribbons. The aroma comes back out your nose as you chew, circular like smoke. What does Donald dream of as he eats them? What is pleasure like for someone who causes so much pain?

On Turkish Delight

These are love. Gelatin, rose water, finely powdered sugar. A proper Turkish delight should be soft to the touch, yielding, and fill your mouth and nose with the scent of a garden cooling at dusk. It should melt on your tongue after the initial bite. It should be so fine that it makes all other candy—particularly American chocolate—seem vulgar by comparison. In color

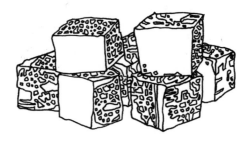

it should be pale pink or maybe slight orange, like an early sunrise reflected on a still, glassy lake.

My first was in an indoor market in Adelaide, Australia, where I studied and fell in love when I was twenty-one. My boyfriend, Rhys, had taken me to the market to buy spices and cheese we'd gain weight on, so deep in sensation that we gave ourselves and each other everything, never thought of consequences, of what we could sustain without changing. That day I stopped at a candy stall, inspecting, always interested in finding things we didn't have back home in the States. I liked the name, and I *did* find them delightful—soft and delicate and shocking. It was a candy made with a flower, like something in a dream, something that doesn't exist out here in the real world, that, upon waking, you wish desperately you could have brought back with you. *How many other things are there like that?* I thought as I stood in the humid rush of bodies, eyes closed, gelatin on my tongue, head full of roses. *How many other loves like this?* I wondered, already knowing the answer.

Before I ever ate it, the dream of this candy was implanted in me by C. S. Lewis's *The Lion, the Witch and the Wardrobe*. The evil queen buys Edmund's loyalty with the most perfect

Turkish delight, and he readily sells out his siblings for this pleasure. He forgets himself, leaves his world behind. As a child I had no idea what this otherworldly treat might be, and all those years later, standing there in the market in the middle of my time with that love, the tale half over without my knowing it, that old story was far from my mind. But months later, when it was nearing the day for me to go back to my country, Rhys proposed that we read to each other from his parents' old set of the Narnia books—small paperbacks with wonderfully psychedelic 1970s artwork, page edges worn velvety. It would be an innocent consolation and a ritual. We told each other these stories, long into those final nights, on the enclosed porch that served as my bedroom, stars and distant city lights and the shadows of eucalyptus just there, beyond the darkened glass. We couldn't wake from the dream, we reasoned, if we never fell asleep. We finished the last book as the sun came up on my final day, then headed directly to the airport. I thought I would return, but I never found my way back.

On Cotton Candy

Cotton candy occurs at the fair, bobble-floating on sticks clutched by tiny, enraptured children or held aloft by dads seeking a clearing in which to dole the thing out to the kids. As the late-fall crowds shuffle along the cleared dirt paths, the unicorn pastels of cotton candy dot the landscape of brown and olive barn coats, dark blue polar fleeces, decommissioned army jackets. It is thrilling to watch the cotton candy attendant (cook? clerk?) twirl that gossamer ball to-gether from within a steel vat, their wrist and elbow practiced and fluid as they make candy out of thin air. Cotton candy is an edible cloud, the purest possible form of sugar, a miracle of physics, and still, I hate it.

I grew up near one of the oldest agricultural shows in America, the Fryeburg Fair (more than a hundred years older than the Moxie Festival). We even had an early October Friday off school for it, built right into the calendar. There were all the standard midway rides—Ferris wheel, teacups, the brain-squishing Gravitron—plus games: darts and balloons, horse racing spurred by squirting water guns, that weirdly cruel game where you throw a ping-pong ball at a bunch of tiny fish-bowls, hoping to land a shiny new pet. All this in addition to the main point of the thing: prize horses and sheep and pigs. Plus tractor pulls and other loud events we avoided. I loved the fair—especially the horse stalls and the classic wooden merry-go-round—and my mother loved it, too. It was tradi-tion, but not the oppressive kind. Added to these man-made amusements was the excitement of the oncoming fall, change hurrying along unbidden. The only stressful part was parking, usually in a cleared field owned by an enterprising neighbor to the fairgrounds, and driving out of there at the end of the day in a long, slow line of cars, many piloted by dads who'd had a few too many plastic-cup beers. Mom would be a bit irritated, but I'd be sated, tired and full of the day, the red and white car lights like constellations soothing me to sleep.

The fair was full of little shots of magic, some of which I didn't understand. I begged for and collected clutches of

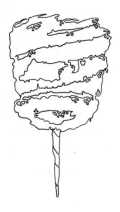

colored feathers on suede straps, gathered together in what I didn't know was a roach clip. I wore them in my hair. There was also a suspicious number of decorated mirrors with high-edged frames, clearly not meant to be mounted on the wall. I hung out at the fair not with friends but with Mom and Dale. I could sense secret knowledge passing between them but didn't know what questions to ask. I just knew that sometimes when I liked an object, I was being strange or funny without meaning to. This was true my whole childhood, including that Christmas I asked for a red leather jacket. Other times, I failed to desire what I was supposed to. My most consistent failure was baby dolls—I had no interest in pretending to be a mother. The adulthood I imitated in my play was about freedom: travel to exotic lands, love affairs, books with my name on them, money. I didn't want to practice subsuming my desires to another, who would then create another and do the same, on down the line for eternity. Somehow this didn't conflict with my appreciation of my mother's deep love for me, her constancy and dedication.

Cotton candy was another childlike thing I was supposed to like. And I did desire it—it was so beautiful, and who doesn't want pure sugar? My mother said no for years, knowing me better than I knew myself, until she gave in. I remember marveling at how light it felt in my hand as I pulled it with the other one and put a shred in my mouth. I appreciated how it changed from solid to liquid in an instant. You didn't have to chew it, but you did have to swallow. I pulled more, did it again, but kept feeling like something else should happen. And I'd spent too much time in homes mid-renovation, and in half-finished basements, not to associate this candy with insulation, thread-fine glass fibers that could kill if eaten. The adults were watching me enjoy it, and suddenly it felt like I was meant to be in Shirley Temple–innocent bliss, but the whole thing fell short. I felt guilty for having wasted Mom's money after years of her knowing this would happen, but now that we were here, she was gracious and encouraging. She was glad to have given me something I wanted, to let me satisfy my curiosity. I let forth big, performative *mmmmm!*s for her benefit. I know I didn't convince her, but I'm glad I tried.

Cotton candy is the bright lights of the midway and the dark, cool hills just beyond, a final, flawed ritual of happiness before winter starts creeping in. It's Mom loving me and giving me what I wanted even when she knew it might disappoint me, and it's Dale smiling and looking on, none of us knowing what was to come. It's Preston asking me what I think of cotton candy, and listening intently while I argue that the purest version of something you love isn't always the best. It's Liz showing up to the coffee shop with those chenpi candies, every time. It's my bodega Snickers man; the Norwegian; Alan Michael and Daniel on the beach, fresh from the dollar store with another surprise. It's Patty, not caring if I never make those Needhams. Like so many other childhood things, cotton candy should be merely joyous but instead reminds me that my days are limited, can melt away in an instant, like candy filaments. Cotton candy is a lovely taunt, a gossamer memento mori. It reminds me to enjoy whatever sweetness I can with those I love before it's too late.

Acknowledgments

This book was a joy to write, mostly because so many kind people supported it. Huge thanks to my agent, Jin Auh, who insisted on seeing my "secret project," and to my editor, Nicole Angeloro, candy person extraordinaire, who immediately understood what I was trying to do. Thanks to the rest of the team at Mariner, especially Liz Psaltis, Kelly Cronin, and Lindsey Kennedy, all of whom have helped spread the candy gospel. To Chloe Foster for the sharp interior design, and to Yeon Kim for the gorgeous cover. Boundless gratitude to Will Palmer, the best copyeditor in the biz and the kindest human. And, of course, to the incredible Forsyth Harmon for the illustrations. Let's make some more mischief soon.

The first draft of this book was written during my residency at the Tulsa Artist Fellowship; thanks especially to Carolyn Sickles and Caroline Chandler, whose work enables a huge community of artists. Liz Blood, I couldn't have gotten through those years without our coffee dates (RIP Hodges Bend). Thanks to so many other Tulsa friends—DeJon Knapp, Karl Jones, Carl Antonowicz, Sophie Goldstein, Hayley Nichols, Jennifer Hope Choi, Ryan Fitzgibbon, and too many others to name—for strength and company and ideas during the wildest time. Thanks to Melissa Lukenbaugh for the dreamiest headshots and for your company during all those heavy lifts.

This book was also supported by my friends and former colleagues at the University of North Texas—thanks especially to Corey Marks for ongoing mentoring and friendship, and to Jeff Doty and Lesandra Botello for being the best possible neighbors and cat godparents to Ziggy. To Daniel Peña and Tarfia Faizullah, forever partners in crime. Thanks to my current colleagues and friends at Colorado State University who've helped me get over the finish line, especially Dan Beachy-Quick, Harrison Candelaria Fletcher, Vauhini Vara, and Sarah Cooper.

For candy context and history, I'm particularly indebted to Samira Kawash's *Candy: A Century of Panic and Pleasure*, and for background reading on the grocery business I relied on *The Secret Life of Groceries* by Benjamin Lorr. Jennifer P. Mathews's *Chicle: The Chewing Gum of the Americas, From the Ancient Maya to William Wrigley* was also indispensable. Sarah Marshall's podcast *You're Wrong About* is hugely influential in much of my thinking, and several episodes of Chelsey Weber-Smith's *American Hysteria* also informed my research.

The list of fellow writers whose support is integral to all my work is far too long to include here, but for now I'm extending special thanks to Kimberly Grey, and, as always, to Marin Sardy and Dale Megan Healey. Thanks also to Leslie Jamison, Casey Plett, Kimberly King Parsons, Emma Eisenberg, Heather Radke, Hilary Leichter, Ada Zhang, Alex Kleeman, and Maggie Millner. Thanks and love forever to Evangeline White, who helps me see ideas when I don't even know I'm having them.

Thanks to all my students, especially Jasmyn Huff, Kendra Vanderlip, and Cicily Bennion—you help my thinking in more ways than you'll ever know. Thanks to all the sweeties who gave me candy while I was working on this book. And to my semi-formal writing communities: the Grind, the Rogue Grind, and Chelsea Hodson's Morning Writing Club. Thanks to Michelle Anderson and the rest of the La Porte Peinte crew for an unforgettable summer.

Much love to my aunts Glenice Russo and Gwendolyn Fontenault. Thanks to Donna Ferrato for her ferocity and inspiration. Thanks to Patricia O'Toole, who is my model for everything, and the rest of my Maine PR team: Joan Leitzer, Kenneth Spirer, and Governor Janet Mills. Alan Michael Parker and the core beach family—Felicia van Bork, Daniel Lynds, Sundi Richard, and Parker—thanks for encouraging these candy rants, and for so much else. Huge thanks and love to the Witt family for their steady support and so many fun holidays. And finally, to Preston Witt—can't believe we're so lucky.

ABOUT

MARINER BOOKS

MARINER BOOKS traces its beginnings to 1832, when William Ticknor cofounded the Old Corner Bookstore in Boston, from which he would run the legendary firm Ticknor and Fields, publisher of Ralph Waldo Emerson, Harriet Beecher Stowe, Nathaniel Hawthorne, and Henry David Thoreau. Following Ticknor's death, Henry Oscar Houghton acquired Ticknor and Fields and, in 1880, formed Houghton Mifflin, which later merged with venerable Harcourt Publishing to form Houghton Mifflin Harcourt. HarperCollins purchased HMH's trade publishing business in 2021 and reestablished its storied lists and editorial team under the name Mariner Books.

Uniting the legacies of Houghton Mifflin, Harcourt Brace, and Ticknor and Fields, Mariner Books continues one of the great traditions in American bookselling. Our imprints have introduced an incomparable roster of enduring classics, including Hawthorne's *The Scarlet Letter*, Thoreau's *Walden*, Willa Cather's *O Pioneers!*, Virginia Woolf's *To the Lighthouse*, W.E.B. Du Bois's *Black Reconstruction*, J.R.R. Tolkien's *The Lord of the Rings*, Carson McCullers's *The Heart Is a Lonely Hunter*, Ann Petry's *The Narrows*, George Orwell's *Animal Farm* and *Nineteen Eighty-Four*, Rachel Carson's *Silent Spring*, Margaret Walker's *Jubilee*, Italo Calvino's *Invisible Cities*, Alice Walker's *The Color Purple*, Margaret Atwood's *The Handmaid's Tale*, Tim O'Brien's *The Things They Carried*, Philip Roth's *The Plot Against America*, Jhumpa Lahiri's *Interpreter of Maladies*, and many others. Today Mariner Books remains proudly committed to the craft of fine publishing established nearly two centuries ago at the Old Corner Bookstore.